WOOD FINISHING

* liming 139 *

WOODWORKER GUIDE

WOOD FINISHING

NOEL JOHNSON LEACH

ARGUS BOOKS

Argus Books Limited
1 Golden Square
London W1R 3AB

ISBN 0 85242 889 8

Phototypesetting by Rapidset and Design Ltd
Printed and bound by Whitstable Litho

CONTENTS

1	History of wood finishing	1
2	Health and safety	4
3	The substrates	11
4	Materials used by the wood finisher	15
5	Abrasives	23
6	Waxes	28
7	Bleaching wood	33
8	Stripping	37
9	Filling grain	45
10	Staining wood	53
11	Shellac	71
12	Varnishing	76
13	French polishing	82
14	Modern wood finishing and spray guns	90
15	Burnishing and pullovering	108
16	Flatting	114
17	Care and maintenance	121
18	Wood eaters	127
19	Floor polishing	132
20	Distressing	135
21	Powered machines	141
22	Suppliers of materials	146
	Index	149

The Author wishes to record his gratitude to the following people for their help in the production of this book:

N. Deborah Mularczyk SRN, SCM, NDN Cert. for medical information on "Skin Complaints" contained in Chapter 3.

Rentokil Ltd., 218, London Road, East Grinstead, West Sussex for special enlarged photographs of wood-boring insects and operators which are used in Chapters 18 and 19.

Mrs. Bristow, Harvest Hill Farm, Blackboys, East Sussex for permission to use photographs in Chapter 20.

Joan Leach, Burwash Place Cottage, Burwash Placé, Spring Lane, Burwash, East Sussex for technical photography throughout and for typing the text.

Front cover photograph courtesy of John Myland Limited (Inc. Gedge & Co.)

HISTORY OF WOOD FINISHING

Wood finishing consists of preserving and colouring. Early man discovered that to use the fantastic supply of wood, growing around him in great abundance, it had first to be cut, shaped and preserved or it would quickly rot and decay. The objects he made included ships, wheels, houses, ploughs, furniture and weapons: all had to have some preservative coating.

The early Greeks, Egyptians and Romans were good wood finishers. The Greeks used crude resins mixed with vegetable oils to daub on their boats to make them waterproof. The Egyptians used shellac (as we now call it) and tar, used as a preservative and as an adhesive, and were also great users of pitch – was it not Pharaoh's daughter who found the baby Moses (Exodus Chapter 2) "daubed with slime and pitch in the flags by the river's brink". It is odd to think that the Jewish nation owes its origins to a wood finish! The Romans also used pitch, tar and waxes for all their wooden implements, weapons and buildings etc. They also used a method called "charring": the exterior surface of wooden beams, posts etc. were charred by flame to produce a coating of charcoal to a depth of about ¼″ which would not support fungi, growth or pests, and would resist rot when put into the ground.

Down the centuries, resins of all kinds were tapped from trees – gum arabic from the Acacia tree found in the Middle East and parts of Africa; turpentine, also a resin, was tapped from the longleaf pine and has been used for making varnish for hundreds of years. Turpentine was carried on most British man-o'-war ships during the 17th and 18th Centuries, mainly for preserving the ship's oak from wood-eating pests, but also for use on wounds.

Shellac, or Lac, was used in various countries throughout the world. Originally from China and India, it was used at first for colouring silks, leather and then later for coating wood. The word "Shellac" is a 19th Century term and is a refined form of lac – a resinous secretion of the lac insect (Laccifer Lacca). Whilst the lac resin was used for thousands of years, it must not be confused with "french polish" as we know it today. The first "do-it-yourself" text-book on wood finishing, *A Treatise of Japanning and Varnishing*, published in 1688, and written by John Stalker and George Parker, often mentions lac in the various formulae given for varnishes throughout the book.

Beeswax, the waste comb construction wax produced by the female worker bee, has also been used for centuries for various purposes. One was to apply warmed wax, made into a polish, to bare wood. This was used to great effect during the Tudor period where simple solid oak furniture was finished with this wax, which during the passage of time and with the help of soot and grime has produced the lovely dark oak patina so prized by antique collectors today.

Wood finishing was also practised, not just for utilitarian purposes but for decorative use on joinery, furniture and wooden weapons with waxes, tar or pitch. The Egyptians in particular brought this decorative aspect to a fine art by applying gold leaf to their furniture, as tomb artefacts have shown us. Indeed, gold leaf decoration is still used today in palaces, stately homes and public buildings.

During the 18th Century turpentine was easily available and this fluid was mixed with beeswax to formulate a finish which was applied with vigour to harpsichords, for example.

When the public demand for harpsichords fell off in favour of piano-fortes, various manufacturers of the time – one being "Broadwoods" went over to a new type of finish called "French polish". From 1815 most manufacturers followed suit, thus replacing the tedious hand finish of turpentine and wax.

French polish, a shellac and spirit based mixture, depended (and still does) upon the skill of the operator. As such it is a commercial art form of wood finish. Until the 1920s and 1930s, french polish was the prime finish for all domestic and commercial woodwork, but in the 1930s cellulose came in and there was an almost universal move over from organically produced finishes to chemically produced ones.

Since the 1930s many cellulose and synthetic surface coatings have been developed and used, and cellulose has now been greatly replaced in its turn by more sophisticated finishes using acids as catalysts. Such finishes, called pre-catalysed, acid-catalysed, polyurethane and poly-ester are all basically branded as lacquers, and these fast-drying sur-face coatings have the advantage of being heat, water, alcohol, acid and alkali resistant – something that french polish never was.

The Victorian period dictated that furniture must be dark and pol-ished to full gloss with the grain of the wood filled. It had a heavy and gloomy look, but today all that has gone. The grain of the wood has been re-discovered and enhanced by modern finishes which are not only gloss but matt and semi-matt, and we also have speckled, splat-tered and pigmented coatings.

Today, these coatings are often applied by robots, by surface coating machines, by spray guns, and last but not least – by hand.

Present-day technology in wood finishing is a highly specialized oc-cupation. The Industry produces many sophisticated surface coatings for joinery and furniture. The operators are skilled in applying these materials and most of them have "gone through the mill" from using traditional finishes to the complicated modern chemical finishes. Why is all this trouble taken to finish or apply a surface coating "film" to wood? Just imagine your dining-room table has been delivered from the cabinet-makers in its raw unfinished state. Very soon the wood would look greasy, dirty, stained and shabby, and the furniture would soon crack or split up. Surface coating with some form of hard drying ma-

terial is applied for the following reasons:
1. To increase the natural beauty of the grain and texture.
2. To facilitate easy servicing or cleaning.
3. To seal the fibres of the wood, thus preventing excess evaporation of the natural moisture content.
4. To obtain a uniform colour and texture to match other woods.
5. To help preserve the wood from wood-eating insects and decay.
6. To minimise the adverse effect of central heating.
7. To increase the resistance of the wood to damages and wear.

Continuing development and constant innovations make prospects exciting for the wood finishers of the future. Probably wood may be treated by infra-red or ultra-violet rays – gamma rays fusing in the natural chemicals in the wood and producing an ultra-hard surface film – but that at the moment is fantasy! To the wood finishers of today the skill of hand-applied surface coatings is still basically the same as it was thousands of years ago, and still has the same purpose – to beautify wood.

HEALTH AND SAFETY

Health risks are encountered in using various products available on the DIY and trade market for finishing on wood. In Industry, these factors are covered by the "Health and Safety Act of 1974" which places a duty upon manufacturers and suppliers as well as the wholesalers and operators who "finish wood", and as far as practicable makes sure that the materials and their usage are as safe as possible when properly used. This act also covers safe working conditions in connection with handling, storage and transport of the materials concerned.

The DIY enthusiast or amateur decorator however is outside the type of practical control of the Inspectorate of this Act of Parliament, although the hazards in the usage of finishing materials are just as acute when amateurs use them as professionals. Troubles frequently occur as a result of lack of knowledge and thought.

The hazards fall into two main categories: fire and explosion, and toxicity. The latter also covers irritants, fumes and dust. In order to outline them and the necessary precautions to be taken in their storage and use, it is easier to deal with each category in turn.

Fire and explosion risks

Fire is the hazard associated with handling and storage. All cans containing flammable liquids carry a flash point label and are classified in three main groups:
1. Flash point below 32° (89.5°F)
2. Flash point in the range 22°C-32°C (71.5°F-89°F)
3. Flash point below 22°C (71.5°F). This type of liquid will be labelled or marked "Petroleum Mixture" giving off an inflammable heavy vapour or "Highly Flammable".

A flash point is the lowest temperature at which the vapour or fumes mixed with air will be ignited by a naked flame. A good guide line is therefore – the higher the flash point the *lower* the risk – the lower the flash point the *higher* the risk. To give one example – nitrocellulose products have a low flash point while raw linseed oil has a high flash point.

New changes in labelling regulations based on directives issued by the EEC commenced in January 1986. The new labelling is to achieve

All containers should be properly labelled

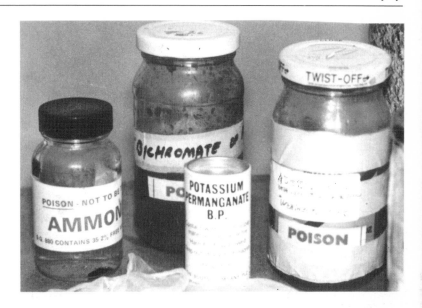

uniformity between member countries of the EEC, to improve information to the customer, and to highlight any particular risk that the customer should be aware of while handling the products.

The new label has four sections:

1. *Symbols.* The warning symbol is black on an orange background. The three symbols involved being (i) the St. Andrew's Cross denoting harmful or irritant; (ii) the corrosive symbol where the product is corrosive; and (iii) the flame symbol where the flash point is less than 21°C.
2. *Indications.* The words "Harmful", "Corrosive", "Irritant" and "Highly Flammable" where applicable are to be used alongside the symbol.
3. *Constituents.* If the product is classified as harmful, irritant or corrosive, then certain substances in the formulation will be shown.
4. *Risk and safety phrases.* These highlight the special hazards of the product and any safety precaution necessary.

The new labelling is a great improvement over the old method. A label now contains a great deal of information. Here is an example:

Makers Name

White Shellac Sealer Ref. No.

Batch No.

Shake well before use

Contains Ethanol 1263 Flashpoint below 21°C

Highly flammable

Keep container tightly closed

Keep away from sources of ignition

No smoking

Do not breath fumes – vapour or spray

In case of insufficient ventilation wear suitable respiratory equipment

5

In case of fire use water spray. Dry powder Co2, sand or earth
Makers name and full address (Flame Symbol)

Fire precautions when working or using flammable liquids

1. Never at any time smoke or have any naked flame such as Calor gas heaters in or near the area of working where woodfinishing products are being used – especially modern cellulose finishing products.
2. Never drink or consume food in a working area while there are fumes floating around.
3. Do not use electrical equipment, such as a power tool, which electrically "sparks" while working with a low flash point liquid or its fumes.
4. Have handy a fire extinguisher (powder type) and also a bucket of sand or an asbestos blanket – if fire starts it takes only a few seconds to be out of control.
5. Have first aid equipment properly and suitably stocked, and handy, with basic materials such as antiseptic creams, eye bath, plasters, bandages, cotton wool etc.
6. Make sure that other people working around know of these hazards by, for instance "No Smoking" signs or other applicable notices.
7. Have no trailing electric cables on the floor from power sanders, spray compressors, drills etc. Have all cables available from central overhead sources.

The storage of fire potential materials and other precautions

1. All bulk stores such as 525 litre cans of cellulose lacquers, thinners, pullover fluids, turpentine etc. should be kept in a separate outside store if at all possible, away from the house or workshop area and in a cool place out of the sun – particularly for bleach containers. If this is not possible, then a metal or concrete container such as a coal bunker or a metal dust bin with a metal lid, once again sited away in a dark, cool corner of the workshop area should be used for bulk storage and with every item clearly labelled. This is far safer than keeping these potential fire hazards on open shelves in or around the home, shed or workshop.
2. Only have sufficient materials for the job in hand in the work area. There is no need to have a 5 litre can of turpentine around if you only require 500 ml for brush cleaning etc. Put it in a small glass bottle with a screw cap instead – properly labelled.
3. Do not keep your normal working supplies of white spirit, methylated spirits, bleaches etc. on shelves exposed to the sun's rays – keep them in a cool place or in the shadiest part of your building.
4. All daily waste materials, such as chemical stripper swabs, sawdust, shavings, teak oil swabs or cloths should be removed from the work area each day. They should be either damped down with water or burned outside in an incinerator, *never* on an enclosed fire in the

house (or in fact any enclosed internal fire). Teak oil swabs or waste will ignite in a confined container so they should be either wetted down or better still, burned outside. N.B. Cellulose waste fluids should *never* on any account be emptied down drains of any description.
5. Label all containers, bottles and tins properly and clearly. A clear liquid could be water, cellulose thinners, white spirit, pullover or spirit – therefore they must be labelled for identification.
6. Keep all wood-working chemicals out of the reach of children.

Toxicity – irritants, fumes and dust

Toxic Fumes

Most chemicals, vapours and gases have some effect on the human system. Some cause anaesthesia; some have positive toxic effects. The following wood-finishing products can give off fumes.
1. Cellulose-based fluids, thinners, nitrocellulose lacquers and their off-springs, precatalysed and acid-catalysed lacquers, pullover fluids etc.
2. Methylene chloride found in most non-caustic paint and varnish chemical removers.
3. Polyurethane varnishes and lacquers (some oil polyurethane varnishes give off isocyanide fumes). These should be clearly marked on the tin by the manufacturer and the most important precaution here is to have adequate ventilation, or the effects of inhaling these fumes can be, at best unpleasant and at worst, positively harmful.
4. Acids and alkalis such as sulphuric acid and caustic soda, used variously in acid finishes, french polishing, and in the case of caustic soda or lye – in stripping wood. These materials must be treated with great care. It must *always* be remembered that when diluting acids and alkalis, *the concentrate must be added to the water* – not the other way round or a mild explosion and spitting will occur.

Irritant fumes

These fumes are unpleasant to the senses and can be harmful to health. They have the effect of dehydrating the membranes of the nose, throat and pulmonary systems. Products such as turpentine, shellac compounded with methylated spirits (although shellac by itself is a non-toxic material), french polishes, oil stains, creosote products and certain wood preservatives and woodworm fluids, all give off these type of fumes.

Precautions to be taken with toxic and irritant fumes

1. See that there is adequate fresh air and ventilation either by open

doors or windows or, better still by extractor fans or air disperse-
ment fans.
2. Wear protective clothing – face or nose and mouth masks.
3. When stripping wood with chemical fluids, wear eye goggles as well.
4. Have a bowl of water handy in case of the accidental spillage of fluids
   on to the skin.
5. After working with these materials, drink plenty of fluids such as
   tea, milk or cocoa.

Dust

Certain woods can cause some operators trouble either with skin complaints or in the respiratory tract, causing asthma due to the inhalation
of organic wood dust. The dust hazard must be kept as low as possible
in any working area – the higher the build-up of chemical dust, the
greater the risk of spontaneous ignition due also to static electricity and
discharge. When finishing wood, the main area of concern is in preparing wood surfaces. The dust can be the sanding waste of the following
materials:
1. Solid woods and veneers – both hardwoods and softwoods
2. Chipboard and blockboard
3. MDF board
4. Plywood
5. Hardboard
   Other sources of dust are from wood sealers and wood fillers and the
use of abrasive papers and steel wool, spray dust when using cellulose
products, particularly acid-catalysed lacquers, and the normal workshop or on-site dust such as brick or concrete dust which is one of
the worst on-site hazards.
   One other source which cannot be ignored when carrying out antique restoration work is from brass polishing. Brass metal dust is a
very unpleasant irritant, and when brass is being cleaned, burnished or
polished a face mask is very important as a precaution against unpleasant side effects.

Precautions to avoid dust inhalation

1. Wear a face mask where possible – at all times during working with
   woodfinishing products, and wear goggles or face shields where applicable.
2. Protective clothing should always be worn – aprons, boiler suits,
   nylon jackets etc. and headwear of some sort.
3. Provide plenty of ventilation or use an extractor fan where possible
   or a variable-speed electric fan to blow away normal workshop dust
   and fumes.
4. Keep the area of work continuously clean, preferably by using suction cleaners at least once a week to give the work area a thorough
   clean-up.
5. If using power sanding tools, use the type with dust-collecting bags.

6. Damp down the working area with a hand water-spray from time to time. This will tend to trap the dust from concrete floors.

Hazards and precautions when using spray guns

Spray guns are becoming more and more popular, particularly in the DIY market, yet there are many hazards for the unwary in using them and great care must be exercised. Below are a few of the main safety factors to follow:
1. Never smoke while using a spray gun.
2. Never spray when any naked flame is near to the operation.
3. Always wear safety masks, goggles and clothing while spraying.
4. Never fool around with a spray gun or aim it at any part of the body.
5. Never place a hand in front of a spray gun, particularly the electric airless type which have a high velocity.
6. Always have plenty of fresh ventilation while using a gun.
7. Do not spray chemical stripper from a spray gun as certain chemicals react with aluminium-galvanized or zinc-coated parts of a spray gun and can cause an explosion. Such chemicals as trichloroethane and methylene chloride must never be used in a spray gun.
8. Always follow the manufacturer's instructions to the letter.

Skin complaints

A common skin complaint, which, when it appears can be an unwelcome and troublesome guest is dermatitis, causing loss of work time and earnings as well as its unpleasant symptoms. It can be avoided if sensible precautions are taken to minimize the risks.

Dermatitis means inflamation of the skin. There are several types but the one most likely to be encountered by the woodworker in a workshop setting is contact dermatitis. It is caused by some natural and synthetic materials which can irritate or damage the skin; this particular type affects eight out of ten sufferers. The condition is characterised by redness, swelling, blisters and a variable amount of itching caused by irritant substances. The skin becomes inflamed and the protective layer of the skin is damaged. The skin feels sensitive and sore – sometimes distressingly so – and for those severely affected it can interfere with hobbies, sports, occupation and life in general.

There are many substances that can cause dermatitis – eg. plants, medicines, cosmetics and clothing. Detergents and chemicals are a very common cause and about half of the cases of contact dermatitis are of the hands. In woodworkers, sensitising dust may cause a rash on the face, neck, hands and forearms (exposed areas). The actual cause may be either a primary irritant or a sensitiser.

A primary irritant is a substance such as lime, which will cause inflammation of the skin on first contact. The rash produced will disappear fairly rapidly if there is no further contact with the chemical. A very common cause is from using cement in the DIY field. Prevention of recurrence is easy once the irritant is recognised, by means of

9

thorough washing after exposure and by wearing special clothing – i.e. gloves.

Sensitisers are a worse problem. The number of exposures needed to cause dermatitis may vary from just one to many. Common sensitisers are dyes (used in textiles) and flour. A baker for example may become sensitised to flour after having worked with it for many years.

If you think you have dermatitis consult your doctor. Questions about work and possible causes will be asked. Patch testing (a standard method investigating cases of contact dermatitis) could be carried out in order to find the actual cause. A sufferer may also need to leave work if the cause is there, but with an enlightened management may be resettled in another department not involving the same cause of dermatitis.

Prevention of contact dermatitis may well be possible in industry with good working conditions, i.e where there are dust extractors and efficient ventilators, and by wearing protective clothing such as gloves when in contact with detergents or chemicals. Rubber gloves themselves can however cause dermatitis in some individuals who are sensitive to rubber.

Barrier creams are important, but unhurried attention to washing and cleaning hands is more important when using possible irritants. Many people who suffer from just dry skin on the hands may well treat this with a good brand of moisturiser or barrier cream available from a chemist.

The condition can be treated but will not be cured overnight and doctor's advice about use of creams etc. must be adhered to as some creams must be used sparingly while others must be applied thickly. Sunshine and fresh air are a helpful treatment and a doctor may prescribe a course of artificial sunlight. Medicines may be prescribed that are taken by mouth and these include antihistamines and antibiotics and occasionally steroid preparations. Skin preparations containing steroids (cortisone) are a common treatment but must be used with strict instructions from a doctor. They are powerful and may produce side effects. They have an anti-inflammatory affect on the skin which is red, itchy and sore. Cortisone creams vary in strength – most doctors will prescribe a weak preparation to try and control the dermatitis and so reduce any side effects of the drug.

Dressings may be needed to cover the area and pastes containing ichthamol may be used. Tar preparations, although an old remedy, are still an effective form of treatment. They are antiseptic and have a healing effect.

These are the main treatments of contact dermatitis and they may need to continue over many months. Dermatitis is a serious skin condition, but onset can be prevented by simple measures.

THE SUBSTRATES

Before applying any type of surface coating to a substrate, whether it be for artistic decoration, or as a preservative or both, it is always advisable to give a little thought as to whether the substrate will be compatible with the surface coating. It is no use, for instance, using a quality exterior varnish on chipboard which is going to be exposed to our English weather because very soon the surface coating and the chipboard would be rendered useless. The various substrates available to the wood finisher are therefore of vital importance, and he must learn to know the feel or texture of the material and its limitations.

Solid woods

Woods converted from trees are generally conventionally defined – as a general guideline – into "Hardwood" from broadleaf trees (deciduous) and "Softwood" from conifers (coniferous), but to a wood finisher this means little as he or she looks upon wood to be sprayed or hand-polished as simply a "surface". It is a curious fact that not all hardwoods are hard (such as lime) and not all softwoods are soft (pitch pine is a hard softwood). The most important thing is that wood – hard or soft – is the most adaptable raw material available to man, and that the different species which inhabit the globe are counted in many thousands. The oak alone has over 300 varieties! Certain woods are better suited for internal use, such as lime, agba, sapele etc., while others such as oak, teak, cedar etc. are better for external use. It is up to the carpenter and wood finisher to use their skills in choosing the correct wood and compatible surface coating.

Veneers

Veneering is the art of cutting thin sheets of exotic woods and applying them to inferior substrates. The Egyptians over 3,500 years ago practised the craft to a fine artistic standard, and during the period of the Roman Empire they were able to cut veneers much thinner due to the invention of the bowsaw. After the fall of the Roman influence the skill was lost for many centuries until its revival in the Renaissance period.

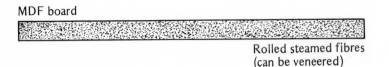

MDF board

Rolled steamed fibres
(can be veneered)

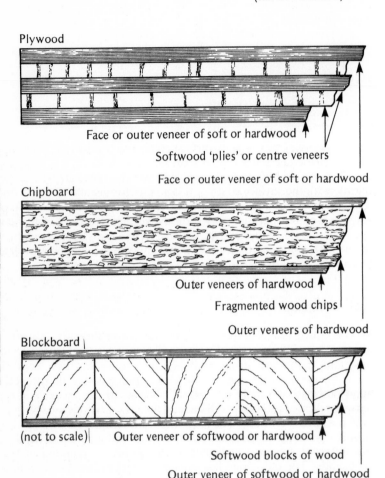

All blocks or veneers set at 90° to the facing panels

Plywood

Face or outer veneer of soft or hardwood ↑

Softwood 'plies' or centre veneers

Face or outer veneer of soft or hardwood

Chipboard

Outer veneers of hardwood ↑

Fragmented wood chips

Outer veneers of hardwood

Blockboard

(not to scale) Outer veneer of softwood or hardwood ↑

Softwood blocks of wood

Outer veneer of softwood or hardwood

By the 19th Century the technique of veneering had come back into fashion in England. Since the invention of the powered circular saw in 1805, and later the powered knife slicer and rotary cutters, veneering has never looked back. Modern veneering technology now cuts to a thinness of paper woods such as oak, ash, yew, rosewood, birch, sapele, walnut, mahogany and many others are produced to adorn the furniture of today and is used on substrates such as chipboard, MDF Board, plywood, blockboard as well as solid woods of inferior grain.

To the wood finisher, veneers have their pitfalls. The repair of veneers on antique furniture for instance is an art, while stripping and resanding must be done by hand or damage can occur. The worst crime an operator can commit to a veneered surface is to "rub through" to the underlying substrate, and great care is also required on older veneers where animal glues have been used. No water in the form of water-washable chemical strippers or water stains should be used or the veneered sheet can "lift" off the substrate. Veneers therefore have to be treated with respect, but they are compatible with any type of surface coating, with the exception of rosewood and teak which require special shellac sealers. Modern veneers are cut basically by two methods: "Peeling the Log" (rotary action) or by a piston powered "knife" (sliced action). The latter method is the one used in mass production of veneers today.

Plywood

The most popular man-made sheeting or boarding is manufactured from solid woods which are veneered and then laminated so that each sheet is lying at 90 degrees to the adjacent one and pressed together using resin glues. Great strength is obtained from this method of pressing and there are a great variety of plywood sheetings: "marine", "building", "interior", "exterior", and various exotic veneers which can be used as decoration. The main advantage of plywood is in its great strength in large sheet forms which is not possible in solid woods. The wood finisher will find a material which is compatible with any wood finish from wax to lacquer provided that adequate sanding sealers or primer coatings are used. Plywood is a material which is used in boat-building, aircraft, furniture, pianos, organs, buildings, toys, TV and film sets and many other purposes.

Blockboard

Blockboard is constructed in a similar fashion to plywood but only three "plies" are used. Two outer veneers, generally of sapele, birch or oak are used to sandwich the centre which is an assembly of solid softwood "blocks" set at 90 degrees to the outer veneers. This boarding is greatly used where large areas of wood are required without bending such as table tops, benches, counters, panelling etc. It does not have the strength of plywood but it does keep its "flatness" better. To the wood finisher there are no problems as any surface coating can be applied to it, but as it is a "thirsty" substrate adequate sanding sealers must be applied to produce a smooth base finish.

Medium density fibre (MDF) board

This is the newest of manufactured boards and was developed in America. It is made from wood but is a new material in its own right and must not be confused with hardboard which is more of a building trade material. Natural wood is reduced to a fibrous state and then, by a combination of steam and mechanical grinding, the fibres are reassembled, dried and impregnated with synthetic resins. The resultant "pulp" is pressed and rolled to obtain thicknesses from 45mm to 6mm.

MDF board can be sawn, planed, machine profiled, turned or carved just like solid wood. The beauty of MDF boarding is that the edges can be shaped by routers, thus eradicating the need for edge banding plantation which is required with plywood, chipboard or blockboard. This boarding is now used by leading piano, organ and furniture manufacturers, but there are two drawbacks: one is the weight of the board and the other the edge damage problem where repairs have to be carried out using special stoppers. To the wood finisher MDF board has had finishing difficulties. The manufacturers improved the water resistance of the product by using waxes in the make-up of the board which caused severe problems to finishing, but this has now been overcome by leading manufacturers of surface coatings who have produced a two-pack sealer for the edges and surface of the board so that the cracking up and "sinking" of finishing films has now been eliminated, and MDF can now be coated with any finishing material.

Chipboard

Chipboard (known as prepared wood) is a most popular man-made board. It is used by the building, furniture, piano and DIY industries. The boards give good strength, are lightweight and consistently flat and are manufactured by fragmenting wood into regular shredded sizes or chips which are then mixed with resin glues and pressed to produce varying thicknesses.

Various qualities of chipboard are produced – the building trade use a much denser quality board for flat roof and flooring requirements. A lighter variety which normally has two outer skins or veneers such as mahogany, sapele, oak etc. is produced for decorative use. There are also pigmented and simulated melamine coated surfaces for kitchen and bathroom purposes or fitted bedroom furniture.

To the wood finisher the only problem is the damages to edges which can sometimes be difficult to repair, but, provided the appropriate sanding sealers are used the material is quite compatible with any surface coating.

MATERIALS USED BY THE WOOD FINISHER

Basic materials used in wood preparation

The preparation of a surface prior to finishing is of great importance. The professional spends over 50 per cent of his time preparing the wood or the surface coating to as near perfection as possible, and the tools that are available are quite simple. There are two main items for hand use: sanding blocks and cabinet scrapers.

The sanding block

This is a piece of rubber, cork or soft wood, preferably with a ¼" felt on the base to cushion the impact of the abrasive papers on the wood. The papers can be used dry or wet as required, depending on the surface being prepared.

The cabinet scraper

In recent years this tool suffered a decline. Some manufacturers dropped it from their range, but have now resurrected it and it is rapidly becoming as popular as ever. It consists of a piece of steel of "saw" quality measuring approximately 5″ x 2½″ which technically has eight

Sanding block

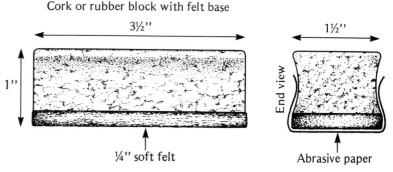

Cork or rubber block with felt base

3½"
1"
¼" soft felt

1½"
End view
Abrasive paper

This sanding block can be made of varying sizes

15

Usage of the sanding block with the direction of the grain

Tools used in the preparation of surfaces

To avoid damage to hand
keep this edge blunt

Saw quality steel

2½"

5"

End view
exaggerated

Two sharp
edges

Cabinet scraper for preparation of wood

Rubber, cork or wood

Felt →

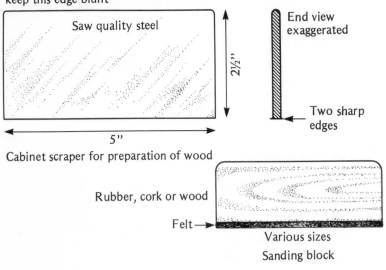

Various sizes
Sanding block

This edge used

Cabinet scraper for stripping surfaces
when using chemical strippers

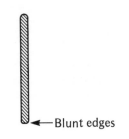

← Blunt edges

cutting edges although in practice two are sufficient on the longest edges. The edges can be produced by filing flat using a fine bastard file, by honing or "turning" with a round-edged tool such as a round-shanked screwdriver or the back of a gouge to produce two turned burrs on the long edge. It is best to have the top edge blunt so as not to cut your hand. The scraper is used by two hands pushing at a slight convex action on to the wood with the direction of the grain – wafer thin shavings are produced.

The purpose of a cabinet scraper is:
1. To remove all machine and tool marks on the surface of the wood.
2. To remove shellac, lacquer etc. from veneered surfaces.
3. To produce a fine, smooth finish on cross-grained woods prior to sanding.

Dusting Brushes

A must in any tool kit – this is a rectangular-shaped brush with a very short handle. The brushes have soft bristles about 2"-2½" long and are used to clean down mouldings etc. between coatings of shellac, paint, varnish etc.

Lining brushes or quills

These brushes have long trailing hairs of 2"-3" in length and are used to impact grain, lines etc. on furniture and coachwork.

Guilders' tips

These are actually very fine camel hair bristles trapped between two pieces of cardboard and their one object is to apply gold leaf to the substrate.

Glue brushes

These have a wooden handle and the bristles are wired in so that when used in a glue kettle (pot) the bristles do not drop out when in contact with hot animal glue.

Beezers

A beezer is a round strip of felt rolled up into a pad and it is used in the french polishing process and described more fully in the flatting chapter.

Brushes

Numerous types of brushes are available to the wood finisher, and one must use the correct type of brush for the particular job. Below are listed a selection of important brushes:

Mops

These curiously are not called "brushes", yet their most important use is that of applying shellac, spirit, varnish etc. They have hairs of squirrel, sable, bear, goat or mixtures and come in sizes from No. 2 to No. 16. A good qualify mop is an expensive item and should be carefully cleaned after use.

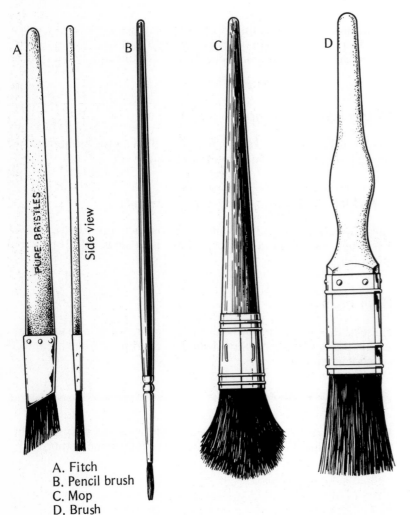

A selection of "brushes"

A. Fitch
B. Pencil brush
C. Mop
D. Brush

Pencil brushes

These are used for touching-in, using pigments, stains, shellac, cellulose etc., and also for fine figure work on simulating veneer grain. They are available in various sizes, the best ones coming from artists' materials manufacturers. The hairs are usually camel (not from the animal but named after the man who produced the pencil brush). They are expensive but worth the money.

A pencil brush being used to 'adjust' the grain on a mahogany table top

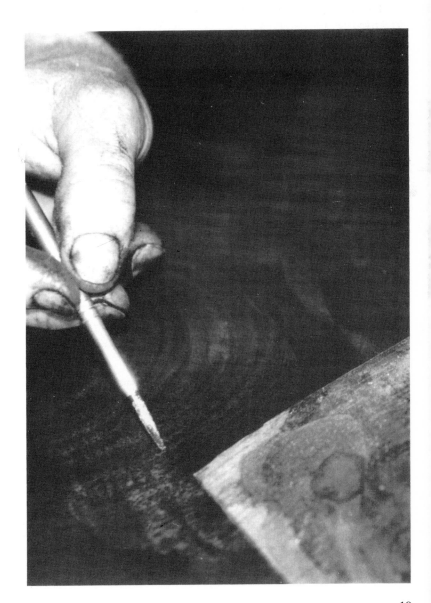

Fitch brushes

These are flat stubby brushes about 8″-10″ in length with a flat wooden handle and bristles of hogs' hair. They come in various sizes and are mainly used for applying shellac polish, stains, varnish etc. to carved work and mouldings.

Stripping brushes

Known as "grass" brushes, they are made from tampico and other vegetable fibres and are light cream in colour. It is important to choose this type of brush for stripping as strong chemicals have no effect on the bristles. They are also used in the bleaching technique on wood.

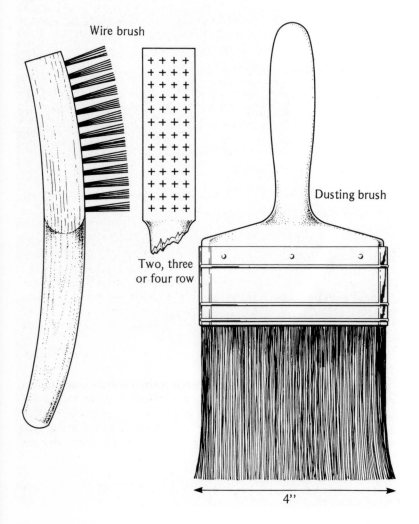

Wire brush

Two special brushes

Two, three
or four row

Dusting brush

4"

Dulling brushes

These are similar to a shoe brush with soft firm bristle hairs about 1″ in length. They are used for applying fine grade dulling powders such as pumice powder.

Wire brushes

These are wooden stock brushes with flexible wire "bristles" in two, three or four rows, and are ideal for:
1. Cleaning our dirt or gunge from carving, spindles etc. or when chemical stripping, or cleaning rust from iron work, hinges etc.
2. Cleaning out dirt in open-grained woods, such as oak, prior to liming.
   The "bristles" can be of steel or brass wire or a mixture of both. Care must be taken not to cross the wood-grain while using these very popular brushes.

Varnish brushes

These must be of the best that money can buy. They come in sizes from ½″-3″. Some are oval, some flat. They are used mainly for applying varnish to top class work, but also on high-class coachwork.

Stippling brushes

These are rectangular-shaped brushes having stiff bristles, which are used for applying stippling pigments on non-absorbent woods.

Rags used in the preparation and finishing of wood

The correct choice of rags during any process in wood finishing is of great importance to the polisher or wood finisher and should be used carefully. Below is a popular range of rags in common use.

Light-weight (7 oz.) hessian is best for applying and wiping off paste woodfiller.

Coloured rags are best used for applying stain and for general dusting for most workshop jobs.

Linen or cotton rags are ideal for french polish rubbers and pullover rubbers used in modern finishing techniques. They must be well washed and free from fibres or lint. Best quality washed linen or cotton must be used for good quality work so that the polish flows through the rags. New rags are quite useless because they carry raw dyes, lint and dressing used in the finishing of the cloth. Traditionally, *sail cloth* is used for quality work.

Washed bleach mutton cloth is ideal for burnishing, for example gloss lacquer finishing, and for waxing.

Tac rags. Sold under the trade name, they consist of folded muslin impregnated with a sticky, slow-drying oil. Used for dusting between coats of lacquer, french polish, varnish or paint. These rags pick up minute particles of dust from the surface prior to spraying or polishing etc. They should be used with care, particularly during cellulose spraying.

Thin unwashed chamois leather can be used to cover the rubber in the pullover process of lacquer finishing. It exerts considerable "bite".

Real velvet (not Dralon). A pad of wadding is covered with velvet and the wadding is saturated with varnish. With this rubber the operator is able to lay on a coat of varnish without brush marks. It requires skill.

French polishers' wadding (not upholstery type). Used for making fads and rubbers for french polishing or staining. Consists of soft non-flattening cotton fibre. White upholsterers' wadding which has a size skin on each side is not suitable for making rubbers. The best type for polishers has no skin at all.

Upholsters' white cotton wool. Used for removing "gunge" when stripping furniture with chemical strippers and for wiping down dirty surfaces. It has excellent absorption.

Stockinette cloth. Normally 2-ply and semi-absorbent, this comes in rolls and is supplied from the mills. It is not recommended for use until it is washed, but is useful as it comes for cleaning down, dusting and for wiping down bleached surfaces etc.

Paper cloths. As white linen is very expensive, cotton sheeting, stockinette, mutton cloth and washed coloured rags, and soft pliable (2/3 ply) paper are now accepted in the home and industrial workshops for mopping up spillages and general cleaning down of surfaces, and cleaning out mops and brushes etc. The most important factor is price. Normally this product is supplied in roll form or on a dispenser, and is a must for any workshop, garage, home or for the do-it-yourself enthusiast.

ABRASIVES

Abrasive materials are important to the wood finisher and glass paper is no longer the only one available. The rapid increase in the use of cellulose-based lacquers and other synthetic finishing materials make it vital to understand the nature of these modern abrasives and how and when to use them.

The most common abrasive substances are coated papers which are used to smooth surfaces and remove imperfections and to key in finishes. They are supplied in either roll disc or sheet form and can be used by hand or by power sanders – belt, orbital or rotary. It is strange that we still use the term "sanders" or "sandpaper" when there is in fact nowadays no such thing! The term goes back in time to when cabinet makers of the day made their own "sandpapers" by coating old papers with animal glues and dipping them in sand or brick dust.

Basically, there are two types of abrasive papers: *Cabinet*, those used on raw wood, and *Finishing*, those used on coated surfaces such as paint, varnish, shellac, lacquers etc.

It is so easy for the novice, or for that matter even some experienced workers, to use the wrong type of abrasive paper. Here are the various types of coating readily available on the British market.
1. Glass or flint
2. Garnet
3. Aluminium oxide
4. Silicon carbide
5. Emery

The grading of abrasive papers is determined at the manufacturing stages by the amount of "grit" used in relation to a specified mesh filtered square centimetre – for example, 100 grade is equal to 100 particles of glass, garnet, aluminium oxide or silicon carbide to each square centimetre.

Glass or flint

These are amongst the oldest kinds of abrasives. They are normally supplied with a light yellow-brown backing colour, animal glues, and fine-to-course glass or flint, which is the abrasive material. The finest grade is "flour". They are used on raw wood and are cheap papers

The author's own abrasive paper dispenser. Note that they are stored face down to keep them free of dust

without much bite. They wear out very quickly and are generally used in the "do-it-yourself" trade as the professional finisher finds very little use for these old-fashioned abrasive papers.

Garnet paper

This is a splendid abrasive paper. It is a tawny-red colour, caused by the "garnet" – a naturally occurring iron/aluminium/silicon amalgam. It is very popular with cabinet makers and joiners, and is used on raw wood. It has a good bite and lasts a long time. The grades range from 40 (rough) to 320 (fine), and the latter grade can also be used in finishing as it is ideal for fine smoothing. It is also excellent for finishing wood-turning and has generally replaced glasspaper in the professional workshops.

Aluminium oxide

These are the newest of abrasive papers. They are made from metallic oxide coatings on strong paper backing and they come in various colours, such as green or brown. They clog up quickly but are specially suited for power sanders due to their very long-lasting qualities and are ideal for all cabinet work and joinery. Grades are from 24 (rough) to 400 (fine).

Silicon Carbide

These are the main papers used by the professional polisher of today. They are extremely fine and sharp and really "cut" when used on surfaces such as shellac, varnish and nitrocellulose finishes. They are produced by high temperature fusing of silica sand and coke, and can be used both on cabinet and finishing surfaces. There are two types available:

Waterproof Silicon Carbide – commonly known as "wet and dry". These are dark grey in colour and have a waterproof backing. They are available in grades from 60 (coarse) to 1200. When used with white soap and rain or distilled water, the combination makes an excellent abrasive. It is non-scratching and can be used for the removal of nibs or cissing from lacquer coatings before using pullover and burnishing waxes or creams. It can also be used dry.

Lubrisil Silicon Carbide. A dry talc-like lubricated paper which is light grey in colour. Unlike other papers lubrisil will not close or lose "teeth", and because it is used dry it ensures that the work also remains clean and dry. Lubrisil is used on fine finishing work – for example car body repairwork, furniture making, paint and varnish, lacquers and fibreglass, and is also ideal for use on the woodturning lathe. It is made in various grades from 80 (coarse) to 320 (very fine).

Emery abrasives

These are used mainly in metalworking – iron, steel, brass etc. and there are two types available:

Emery blue cloth backing – a tough abrasive with fine to coarse grades.

Emery white cloth backing – a tough abrasive with fine to coarse grades but cheaper than the blue back.

These are worth mentioning because in furniture restoration work there are often castors, hinges etc. which require cleaning.

Pumice powders

These are made from lava deposits and are supplied in various grades, the fine ones being used by the wood finisher. Pumice powder is also used with a beezer in the flatting technique.

Rottenstone

This product (sometimes known as Tripoli Powder) is very much finer than pumice powder. It is a siliceous limestone powder used as a fine burnishing agent for use in creams and pastes and is mainly used for burnishing nitrocellulose finishes. It can also be used with wax polish to provide a useful reviver for french polish.

French chalk

This is an acid magnesium metasilicate – a talc-like powder used as a very mild abrasive in creams, revivers, haze removers etc. It is also sometimes used as a lubricant on dancefloors, table slides (wood to wood), piano actions and occasionally as a filler for oak open grain.

Vienna chalk

A form of precipitated chalk, off-white in colour and soft in texture, which contains magnesia. It has one purpose to the wood finisher – as a final remover of surplus oil in conjunction with mild sulphuric acid in the acid finish technique in french polishing.

Steel wool

This is another important abrasive material indispensible to the wood finisher as it is widely used in both traditional and modern polishing techniques. It is produced in various grades:

0000 and 000 for fine work, dulling varnish or french polish, or to achieve an antique finish when waxing wood.

00 and 0 – for general household use and for rubbing down paint/varnish work in the preparation stages.

No 1 and 2 – for cleaning machinery or tools and for smoothing down first coat paint or varnish.

No 3 – for removing rust from metal, paint or varnish.

No 4 and 5 – for rubbing down parquet floors, for use with strippers on chair spindles and for general stripping of furniture.

On wood, the wool is used dry when no finish has been applied. For stripping surfaces, the wool is used with liquid chemical stripper. For household use, the wool is used with soap and water.

Waxes and creams

The last of the abrasive materials available to the wood finisher are the abrasive waxes and creams. These are called burnishing waxes with added abrasives such as pumice or rottenstone with a little carnauba wax. Sometimes a little ammonia is also added. They are excellent burnishing agents for use on gloss nitrocellulose when a mirror gloss is required. Best results are obtained when these burnishing materials are used with power polishing machines or by hand with washed mutton cloth.

A useful dispenser for steel wool which can be cut with scissors to reduce wastage

WAXES

Beeswax

It is an interesting fact that the wood finishing trade depends entirely on the by-product of two insects – both female. One is the lac scale beetle, the "Laccifer Lacca", from which shellac is produced. This is described in detail in the shellac chapter. The other insect is the bee, which provides beeswax. This substance is one of the little miracles of nature for which there is no real synthetic substitute. Beeswax is an animal wax produced entirely by the female worker bee. The wax is non-toxic and is harmless to the skin, and is one of the most important waxes used by the wood finisher. It is used in various composite forms as well as in its natural state. It is a solid wax, fairly hard and with a texture like soap. Beeswax, like honey, is produced by the worker female bee which secretes a special wax that is used to make combs and sealers for the comb ends (called "cappings") to stop the honey from running out to waste. The combs are hundreds of little passages designed for the storage of honey, and when the honey is harvested these combs and cappings are melted and separated from the honey – the bee keeper has therefore two cash crops – honey and beeswax. The melting point of beeswax is 140°F. The raw beeswax is strained, cleaned and refined, poured into clean moulds and allowed to set. The best beeswax is a fine deep buttercup-to-primrose colour with a good aroma.

In this natural state, beeswax has been used for hundreds of years and the early makers of furniture were quick to use the wax for polishing wood and leather. Today beeswax furniture polish is used extensively throughout the antique trade and on some modern quality reproduction furniture. In addition the wax is used as a stopper for small cracks, chips, holes and blemishes on shellac surface work. The wax can also be obtained in bleach form to produce a neutral colour for use on pale coloured timbers such as pinewood, but the bleaching process makes the wax harder and less supple to use. In this state it is sometimes called white beeswax.

Many furniture waxes and creams use beeswax as a part ingredient and it is of interest to note that the wax is also widely used in industry and trades as varied as sail-making, car manufacture (where it is sprayed inside door frames to prevent corrosion), and in pharmaceutical products. It is also used in the manufacture of church candles.

The use of beeswax polish on antiques

While beeswax polish is expensive in today's market place, it can be made by the amateur very easily. To produce a "home-made" furniture wax polish, take a medium-sized pan and into it place a 1 lb. 12 oz. tin (or similar). Pour water into the pan until it comes about half-way up the tin, put the pan on the stove and bring the water to the boil. Turn the heat down so that the water continues to boil gently and into the inner tin place about a quarter of a pound of beeswax and allow it to become liquid. Slowly and carefully add about half a cup of pure (not subs) turpentine and stir in with a wooden spoon to mix well, and then add about a thimbleful of very strong ammonia (.880 type, not the household one), and about a thimbleful of either pumice powder (fine) or rottenstone both of which are abrasive materials which will give the polish just that little "bite". If you wish, you can also add a little carnauba wax to the brew to make the polish shine easier. Mix together thoroughly with your wooden spoon, then turn off the heat and allow to cool. When set take a small sample and try polishing a piece of polished wood. If the polish is stiff, add a little extra turpentine and ammonia. If it's too runny, add a little more beeswax and so on until you have the right consistency – in either case re-heat and mix in. You could also add a little colour (say brown umber) or a little perfume. When you are satisfied with your "brew", pour it off into a nice clean tin with a lid through a sieve and leave to harden off.

NOTE: Remember that all the materials you are using are flammable so take care during the mixing process. It is far safer to do this process outdoors (say with a camping stove).

Carnauba wax

This is another very important wax used by the wood finisher. It is yellowish, non-toxic and harmless to the skin, but differs from beeswax in many ways. First of all it is a vegetable wax – a natural exudation gathered mainly from the Brazilian palm tree at a rate of approximately 6 oz. per tree per year. Secondly it is a very hard wax – so hard that you need to break it into smaller pieces by using a hammer (just like breaking treacle toffee), and with a melting point of 180°F it is without doubt one of the best hard waxes. It is ideal for use on the turner's lathe for final finishing, to spindlework for instance, by using a fast lathe speed and holding the wax against the work lightly but firmly when the friction will melt the wax. This can be followed by 240 garnet papers to provide a super-fine grain-filled hard wax finish. It can be melted and used as a stopper for large areas (for example around knots in pine). It can be incorporated with other waxes such as standard furniture waxes, burnishing pastes and creams, and other polishes and creams which need to be harder and less sticky for cellulose and synthetic finishes. For instance, it is used in most car polishes for lacquer surfaces. Carnauba is supplied in two grades – fatty grey and prime yellow, which is the better quality.

Japan Wax

This originated in Japan but is not really a true wax like beeswax or carnauba, but a blend of vegetable fats with other products such as pigments or shellac. When blended with shellac it makes an excellent stopper, which does not shrink, is hard and which takes french polish or lacquers over it. A "shellac stick" is made in this way, and is the same size and shape as a piece of sealing wax, and comes in a variety of colours – white, black, brown, red, cream etc. so that scratches or imperfections can be filled with the same colour as the surrounding timber. It must be used with a very hot knife to melt the stick – never a match which will simply cause carbonation and blacken. In a modern finishing technique, a cellulose wax is classed as a Japan wax and is used as a stopper in the same way.

Shellac sticks come in boxes of assorted colours and are ideal for the journeyman-polisher where quick repairs can be made to small faults in furniture on site.

Paraffin wax

This is a mineral wax, derived from the petrochemical industry, which is made from paraffin oil (either white or clear), and is commonly used throughout the trade. It is a fairly solid, soft white clear wax and is used, mostly in combination with other waxes, to produce a soft furniture polish. The fact that the wax has "non-slip" properties means that it is frequently used in floor polishes, and, last but not least, it is cheaper than beeswax polishes. It is easy to identify a cheap wax polish by the smell – it has a paraffin odour.

Wooden floors and linoleum are still best polished by wax and with modern electric floor polishers it is so much easier nowadays. A useful way in which paraffin wax can be used directly is to rub it on the slides of drawers if they are inclined to stick slightly.

Other waxes

The following rather strange-sounding waxes are also used in the manufacture of various polishes, frequently as substitutes for beeswax and carnauba waxes, and used in combination with them as a Japan wax.

Candelilla wax

A vegetable-type wax originating from a Mexican plant with a melting point of 150°F.

Ceresin wax

A hard wax which is man-made from a blend of paraffin wax and other synthetic waxes such as ozokerite.

Chinese wax

A wax which insects secrete on to the twigs of the chinese ash tree.

Bleached montan wax

Another man-made product manufactured from brown coal or peat and used as a substitute for carnauba.

Ozokerite wax

This sounds Russian, but is a petroleum extract and is used for blending with other waxes.

Lac wax or shellac wax

Lac wax is basically a hard wax similar to carnauba wax and is a by-product of the process of bleaching and thus dewaxing shellac. It is mainly used in the production of shoe polishes and thin furniture creams. As far as wood and leather are concerned lac wax is used at times as a substitute for carnauba, candelilla or montan waxes, but unlike carnauba, lac wax is not consistent in quality and varies from different growing areas.

Silicone waxes

This is a special kind of wax which has outstanding water repellency and hardness. These waxes are not true waxes but fluids chemically added to various waxes. Silicones are complex in their production and a great variety of both natural and synthetic waxes are used as "carriers" for silicones. Many silicone waxes are on the market in paste, cream and aerosol forms, but they can create considerable problems for the woodfinisher as they "plant" onto the surface of a substrate a "secondary" surface which builds up with the passage of time, and can eat into a surface coating. Great care is needed in applying these silicone waxes. Steel wool however must never be used in conjunction with them as the wool tends to break up the secondary finish.

BLEACHING WOOD

Although it is not greatly used by large finishing concerns, bleaching wood is a very important process to the jobbing wood finisher and antique restorer and must be carried out in a controlled manner. It must be emphasized that bleaching can only be carried out on the natural surface of the wood – surface coatings must first be removed by normal, stripping techniques and allowed to dry out.

Why do we bleach wood?

The answers are varied:
1. To change the natural tone of the wood – that is to lighten dark woods like walnut, oaks, mahogany.
2. To remove stains such as ink, rust marks, ingrained dirt, water marks and spirit stains.
3. To age new veneers prior to refitting for antique furniture repairs.
4. To unify the colour of varying woods prior to staining.
5. To distress colour, particularly in reproduction furniture.
6. To lighten pine furniture after stripping in caustic soda – as caustic soda darkens pine.

The bleaching of wood takes place by a process of oxidation or by the reaction of hydrogen with the chemicals contained in the wood whereby the colour of the wood is changed. For example, if you were making a chest of drawers and had two similar mahogany type woods such as Paldao and Agba, then to obtain a uniform colour a slight bleaching might be advisable so that on staining the overall result would be similar.

If the process is carried out during the summer months, the sun has also a natural bleaching effect upon the substrate and therefore enhances and increases the effect. Some woods however will not respond to bleaching, even when using the strongest of chemicals, and these are frequently the close-grained woods. Those unsuitable for bleaching include Burmese teak, cedar of Lebanon, cedar – western red, ebony, rosewood, eucalyptus or zebrawood. In particular, cedar, teak and rosewood are chemically active and can cause problems to the wood finisher, and bleaching of these timbers is not recommended. Woods that are easily bleached are generally open-grained and include oak, ash, elm, sycamore, beech, mahogany and pine.

Bleaches suitable for wood finishing

1. *Ordinary household quality bleach (chlorinated lime)*. This when dissolved in water is an ideal milder type of bleach for such woods as sycamore and beech.
2. *Oxalic acid*. A mild bleach, but a traditional one for french polishers. It is supplied in powder/crystal form and a good "mix" is 1¼ lb. of crystals to 5 litres of hot water. This bleach is ideal for removing ink stains, rust marks in oak made by iron nails and screws, and stains of all kinds.
3. *Sodium hypochlorite*. A stronger bleach than oxalic acid which, if used neat, will lighten most woods.
4. *The 2-pack Alkali and Acid solution method of bleaching*. This is now the most common method of bleaching used, and consists of two plastic bottles of solution. The first bottle is called literally "Solution A" or "1" and is a strong alkaline such as caustic soda or ammonia which, "degreases" the wood. It is left on for approximately 20 minutes. The second bottle – Solution "B" or "2" is a very strong acid such as hydrogen peroxide which is applied onto the still-wet solution "A" on the substrate, when a "foaming" action will take place. Allow this alkaline/acid reaction to continue for at least 2/4 hours before washing over the substrate with plenty of clean water and then leaving to dry.

Tips for good bleaching

1. Wear old clothes with a protective apron made from rubber. Also a good strong pair of gauntlet rubber gloves, goggles and gum boots.
2. Carry out the whole process out of doors, near a grid with good drainage. Do not attempt this process near grass or foliage.
3. Apply the bleach solutions by a grass brush or any cheap disposable paint brush. (A "grass" brush is made of tampico and other vegetable fibre and is resistant to strong chemicals).
4. Have a semi-hard old-type scrubbing brush handy (not the nylon type).
5. Have a hose pipe with spray attachment connected to a good source of clean water. All traces of bleach must be removed.
6. Have a bucket of water handy in case of accidental spillage of bleach onto the skin. It must be washed off immediately or severe burning will result.
7. Have a glass jar as a container to hold the bleach when applying by grass brush.
8. Store all bleaches in a cool dark place – do not store in sunlight or the contents may expand and explode.
9. If table tops are to be bleached, make sure that the spare leaves of tables are cleated underneath (i.e. a piece of wood screwed down across the grain). This prevents bowing during washing down with water.
10. Do not fool around with bleach. The chemicals are toxic and dangerous and must be treated as such. Do not have children or pets anywhere near, whilst using.

Washing down with running water

Bleaching technique – the two-pack method

Substrate – any solid wood suitable for bleaching. Normal precautions to be taken as previously described.

1. Strip off all old polish and allow to dry.
2. Apply "A" bleach solution by grass brush. This must be carried out very carefully making sure that every inch of wood is treated. Allow to "eat in" to the wood for about 20 minutes.
3. Apply "B" bleach solution by grass brush, again making sure that every part is covered. A "foaming" reaction will take place and this must be kept moist during the period that bleaching is taking place, that is from 2-4 hours (or longer if required), by simply adding more bleach "B", to sustain the moisture.

   NOTE: At no time during this technique will you actually see the bleached effect when the wood is wet – only when the wood has dried out will the full effect be shown.
4. Neutralizing. Use a hose pipe with a fitted spray end unit connected

to a water supply with good pressure. Wash down the substrate for 5-10 minutes, at the same time giving it a good scrub with a small medium soft scrubbing brush (not nylon or plastic). Leave off and allow to stand for five minutes and then repeat the washing down process.
5. Wipe down with a muslin cloth and allow to dry off. If this process is carried out in winter, place the substrate in a very cool room to dry out slowly. If however the job is done in the summer, leave in the sun and drying should be complete in about an hour. The sun will also aid the bleaching effect.
6. When dry, sand down to flatten the grain using 100/240 grade abrasive garnet papers.
   The item is now ready for finishing.

Removing deep stains from solid wood furniture

It.is not recommended that the following technique be used on veneered surfaces which have animal glues for adhesive.
1. Remove all surface coating, such as french polish, lacquer etc by either chemical stripper or cabinet scraper. If chemical stripper has been used neutralize with water or white spirit and allow to dry out.
2. Damp down slightly with water the stained area and apply oxalic acid in fluid form, preferably hot, using an old pencil brush with a dabbing action rather than a brushing one. Leave for 20-30 minutes, and repeat as often as necessary for the stain to be eradicated.
3. When all traces of the stain have gone, wash down with clean water using an old toothbrush to scrub into the grain. Wipe down and allow to dry out.
4. Sand down using 240 grade garnet paper. The substrate will now be ready for refinishing.

STRIPPING

A great deal of mystery hangs over one of the most unpleasant processes which a woodworker has to deal with. It involves the removal of a hard surface film, such as paint, varnish, french polish or one of the various modern lacquers. However if this process is handled properly, following my guide lines, stripping wood can become a great deal more acceptable.

There are many different types of products on the market today for stripping a variety of surface films from wood. In order to choose the correct product, it is necessary to understand the two terms which categorise the different types of finishes. They are *reversible* and *non-reversible* finishes.

Reversible finishes

A reversible surface film can be dissolved in its own solvent and thus revert back to its pre-solution form – for instance, methylated spirits will "reverse" or dissolve standard shellac finishes such as french polish; cellulose thinners will "reverse" nitrocellulose finishes; and turpentine will "reverse" wax or oil finishes.

In general, these finishes can be categorized as follows:
1. Shellac, french polishes, sealers.
2. Nitrocellulose, clear and pigmented, satin or gloss.
3. Wax and oil.

These finishes are reversed using the original solvent with which they were mixed.

Non-reversible finishes

These are finishes which have usually undergone chemical molecular changes in the drying of the film and cannot be reversed back using their own original solvent. A pre-catalysed lacquer, once dry, will not reverse even using the cellulose solvent with which it was originally mixed. Wood glues such as PVA are again a good example of non-reversibility. These non-reversible surfaces are mainly the modern off-shoots of cellulose lacquers and are used extensively in furniture and joinery finishing today. It must also be remembered that oil paint and oil resin varnishes are non-reversible finishes as, once dry, they will not dissolve in their solvent.

These finishes will *not* reverse or dissolve using their original solvent.
1. Resin Oil Varnish and Oil Paints
2. Pre-Catalysed Cellulose Lacquers
3. Acid-Catalysed (2-pack) Cellulose Lacquers
4. Polyurethane (2-pack) Catalysed Cellulose Lacquers
5. Polyester (Wax-type 2-pack) Lacquer

It is first necessary therefore, to identify a surface before attempting to strip it. French polish or nitrocellulose, wax and oil – the reversibles – are easy to recognise, but it is extremely difficult to tell whether a surface is a pre-catalysed or a polyurethane film.

It is of great help if you know the age of the item, for you can then use a general guide to the type of surface film most likely to have been applied. All furniture before 1800 would have been waxed or oiled. Between 1815 and 1930, furniture was generally finished with french polish (Broadwoods, the piano manufacturers, turned entirely to french polish in 1815), and from the 1930s onwards cellulose was used by most manufacturers. Since the 1960s sophisticated catalysed finishes have been used, with developments still going on to improve their drying times and hardness. Water-based lacquers are now being developed and perfected. These are, however, only general guide-lines as changes took place gradually and some manufacturers were prepared to be more adventurous than others in trying new finishes.

To make a more positive identification, try the following tests on an obscure part of the piece of furniture:

To Identify	Test
French polish or shellac surface	(a) Chip off a small piece or scratch with fingernail – a slight dent will be made.
	(b) Rub with a small amount of methylated spirits on a rag – a deposit will be shown on the rag.
Wax or oil surface	Rub with a small amount of turpentine on a rag – a deposit will be shown on the rag.
Nitrocellulose finishes	Rub with cellulose thinners on a rag – the surfaced film will soften quickly.

If these tests show NOTHING on your rag, then you can reasonably assume that the surface is a non-reversible finish. In this latter group, polyester gloss lacquer is easily identified by its "glass" plastic gloss finish, and my advice here is for the amateur to leave well alone – stripping this type of surface is best left to a professional. It is an extremely difficult coating to remove and requires special extra-strong chemical strippers.

Why do we strip?

No finish will last for ever. Outside surfaces have to stand up to sun, rain, hail, frost, condensation, acids, salts, algae and expansion and contraction of the wood due to the extremes of weather during the summer and winter. Interior surfaces have to stand up to high and low extremes of temperature from central heating, condensation, acids (in food), children, general wear and tear, removals, storage and frequent misuse – all of which can lead to broken or chipped surfaces, blisters, burns (cigarettes), heat rings and bleach marks caused by spirits – acids and alkalis.

After identifying the surface finish – that is establishing the reversibility of the surface, I would suggest the following basic procedures.

Stripping reversible finishes

1. French polish and shellac surfaces
If no silicon waxes have been used, this surface can be removed by using methylated spirits or cellulose thinners. If silicone waxes have been used then a standard chemical stripper will be required, but take care with any veneers – do not use a water-washable type of chemical stripper on veneered surfaces.

2. Oil or wax surfaces
This is one of the easiest surfaces to remove by using either white spirit (turpentine substitute) or a good turpentine with 000 steel wool to "scrub" in. Wipe off using cotton waste.

3. Nitrocellulose lacquers
These surfaces can be removed by using a proprietory chemical Methylene Chloride non-caustic stripper. Do not use a blow-lamp or heat gun on these finishes or fire will result.

Stripping non-reversible finishes

1. Paint and varnish for general joinery
This is best removed by using a blow-lamp or hot air gun – the latter being quite easy and safe to use.

2. Paint and varnish for furniture
Use a proprietory chemical methylene chloride non-caustic stripper of either the fluid or paste type. If veneers are involved then care is required, and it may be sensible to use the dry method on these parts.

3. Other non-reversible finishes except polyurethane and polyester
Once again a proprietory chemical methylene chloride non-caustic stripper will remove the surface, but polyurethane and polyester both present special problems and require special chemical strippers.

In all cases please read and follow the instructions on all chemical strippers as they vary from one manufacturer to another, and always remember to neutralize afterwards using the recommended fluids which are usually white spirit, methylated spirits or water.

Methods of stripping

Dry method

(a) With a cabinet scraper (a piece of tool steel approximately 5″ x 2½″) which has for the most convenient use two sharpened edges. It is used in the direction of the grain to remove old varnish or french polish, and is particularly useful for removing polish from veneered surfaces which have been stuck down with reversible animal glues.
(b) With abrasive papers, which can also be used on softer surfaces like shellac. The most suitable are 80 grade Garnet or Aluminium Oxide papers. Care is needed not to "rub into" any veneers present. These papers are also produced for use with power sanders, but these should not be used on veneered or quality furniture as they tend to cut across the grain. Power sanders are however useful for painted surfaces such as panels, doors etc.

A great deal of dust is produced with any dry method and it is recommended that a face mask is worn during the process.

Heat method

This method has become popular recently since Black & Decker and other well-known manufacturers introduced the popular electric Hot Air Gun which is used to heat up the paint or varnish film and then, using a scraper to remove the "gunge" – a mixture of the original surface coating in melted form. A blow lamp has been used for many years by professional decorators for the same purpose, and in recent years, butane gas has replaced paraffin or petrol as the fuel. The heat method is ideal for removing paint and varnish, but care must be taken to avoid burning the wood under the various layers of paint.

Chemical method

Non-caustic chemical strippers have become very popular in recent years and come in two basic forms:
1. A thin fluid – ideal for horizontal surfaces or mouldings and neutralized by white spirit.
2. A thick paste – ideal for vertical and overhead surfaces and neutralized by either white spirit or water (described on the tins as "water-washable").

These strippers mainly contain methylane chloride, which, while safe to use is nevertheless toxic. Instructions on the tins or bottles must be carefully read and strictly carried out. Avoid using the water-washable type on a veneered surface or the veneers will loosen.

Procedure for chemical stripping

1. Stand item to be stripped on various layers of old newspapers.

Applying a chemical stripper by brush

Stripping off the softened surface with a cabinet scraper (end edge)

2. Apply strippers by dabbing brush action and leave on for about 15 minutes. Re-apply using a liberal amount and leave for a further 15 minutes or more, to allow the chemicals to do their job of eating into the hard surfaces.
3. Scrape off surplus by using a blunt cabinet scraper end.
4. Scrub over the surface using coarse wire wool.
5. Wipe off waste using waste cotton wool (upholstery type white cotton wool is ideal for this job).

Scrubbing in the chemical stripper using No. 4 grade steel wool

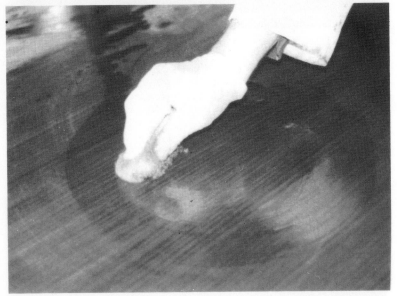

Wiping off 'gunge' using cotton waste with cellulose thinners. Note the use of gloves

6. Use a brass type wire brush to scrub out surplus from mouldings or a sharp wooden stick like a large tooth pick to clear corners (called a quirk stick).
7. Wash all over with cheap cellulose thinners to remove all traces of gunge from the grain.
8. When dry, sand down using 100 grade garnet abrasive papers.
9. Wash down again using methylated spirits, white spirit, cellulose thinners or water (as recommended by the manufacturers of the stripper) to neutralize.
10. Leave to completely dry out. This is very important and at least 6-12 hours is advisable.

Hazards in using chemical strippers

It must be emphasized that the following basic precautions should be taken.

1. Always wear face masks, goggles and proper clothing such as an apron or nylon coat.
2. Always have plenty of ventilation in the work area or better still, do the work outdoors – remember most chemical strippers are toxic.
3. Use a barrier hand cream and gloves – thin canvas ones soaked in linseed oil are better than rubber gloves which soon deteriorate.
4. Do not smoke or eat near work area.
5. After each work session wash hands thoroughly using a coal tar soap to avoid dermatitis, and then apply a medicated hand cream.
6. Have a bowl of water handy in case of accidental spillage on the skin.
7. When using a blow-lamp, it is useful to have either a bucket of water or a small fire extinguisher handy in case you set fire to the wood.

Caustic soda or lye (Sodium Hydroxide) method

This method has become very popular in recent years and therefore must be mentioned. As it is a dangerous and messy procedure, it is best left to the professionals – most towns have good "pine stripping" companies who give a good and reasonbly priced service. It is excellent for removing many layers of paint from doors etc. but can cause problems with some items of furniture because the process softens animal glues and can weaken or loosen joints, and will darken pine. Caustic soda can be purchased in granular form from most DIY shops – usually as a drain cleaner and can be used either with cold water in a bath into which the item to be stripped is dipped, or with hot water in a more concentrated form and applied directly to the wood. Anyone attempting to use this method must remember that they are using a very strong alkali which can cause serious burns to the skin, and therefore great care must be taken in handling it. Strong rubber gloves, goggles and protective clothing including gum boots must be worn at all times, and the work must be carried out preferably out of doors, or if this is not possible, then in a very well ventilated room. When stripped, the item must be washed down (by hose pipe if possible) with plenty of water and left to dry. Caustic soda darkens pine which then requires bleaching if a lighter colour is required.

When mixing the caustic soda, always add the CAUSTIC SODA to WATER – NEVER the other way round as the mixture will boil and spit. The average mixture for stripping is 1¼ oz. of caustic soda to 5 litres of water.

There are always new stripping products coming onto the market which are supposed to strip off any surface coating from wood – some are successful, some are not.

One entirely new commercial method for stripping lacquers, varnish etc. is by the Powered Compressed-Air Bead Glass Blaster, which under fantastic pressure bombards the substrate with dry powdered glass. The advantage of this method is that the whole process is carried

out dry, and that joints are not affected, so refinishing can be undertaken immediately after blasting. The disadvantage of this system is
the high cost of the equipment, and that for health and safety the
operator must be enclosed in a suit and safety helmet with its own inde-
pendent air supply. This method of stripping is obviously therefore
destined only for commercial use.

The fact remains that all stripping is very expensive in both labour
and materials and is indeed a very messy process. It is essential that all
traces of the residues of stripping are removed from the grain and surface of the wood before refinishing takes place. In spite of all precautions, problems in refinishing can still be encountered, such as
cissing (the sprayer's enemy) when using cellulose lacquers. It is therefore advisable to apply one coating of a de-waxed shellac sealer to act
as a buffer coat between the stripped surface and the new refinishing
surface coating.

FILLING GRAIN

When working with wood-finishing materials, the term fillers refers basically to "grain wood fillers". A filler is usually a thin paste which is spread on to the raw or bare wood surface and rubbed well into and across the grain, the residue being wiped off. The object is to choke the pores of the wood in order to prevent greater absorption of surface coating materials such as varnish, cellulose, french polish etc. Fillers may have added pigments of colour so that the filler in the grain matches the wood being worked on.

Traditional french polishers use plaster of paris which eventually shows up white when natural bleaching takes place and the effect becomes unsightly.

Wood fillers consist of:

1. Filling powder: plaster of paris, ground silica, chalk etc.
2. An extender: powders such as china clay which give texture.
3. A binder: determines the type of woodfiller – either oil, resin or catalyst classification.
4. Pigment or colour: bituminous pigments, dyes or stains.
5. Solvent or medium: oils such as turpentine, white spirit, resin, naphtha or other synthetic solvents.

A filling material therefore has to be hard yet easily sanded down and consist of chemically-inert fine particles. It must not interfere with the film-forming fluids which will ultimately lie on top of the fillers – for instance some fillers used under nitrocellulose finishing materials are not compatible with pre-catalysed or acid-catalysed finishes yet are completely compatible with traditional finishes.

Oil bound fillers

Those in which the binding solvent is linseed oil, white spirit, turpentine, gold size, alkyd or synthetic oils. They are called "patent" fillers which are slow-drying and very easy to apply. They have good "slip" and are ideal for shellac-based products such as french polish, varnish etc.

Resin bound fillers

These are much quicker drying and are the solvent or medium used mainly with lacquers of the cellulose and synthetic type. They do not have the "slip" and ease of application of oil bound fillers. Resin bound fillers were also designed to be used under catalysed lacquers and they consist of a fully polymerised filler which produces maximum stability and excellent adhesion. They are not, however, suitable for use under polyester or polyurethane lacquer polishes.

Catalysed fillers

These are very specialist fillers based on synthetic compounds and thinners consisting of easters, ketones and hydrocarbons (see below). These are ideal for acid catalysed and polyurethane lacquers. Some of these terms are explained as follows:

Easters The result of the reaction or an acid and alcohol under heat.

Ketones Very strong solvents for nitrocellulose products such as acetone.

Hydrocarbons These are basically white spirit, paraffin, turpentine, coal tar solvents such as xycol, naphtha, benzol, toluol and are all used extensively in the make-up of modern finishing products.

A new range of fillers has recently appeared on the market classified as "thixotropic wood fillers", which are compatible with most finishes and are easy to use. They are a thick jel paste which when rubbed onto wood and exposed to the air become fluid and spread easily.

A "substrate" (a new word not found in many dictionaries) means in finishing jargon the actual type of wood – chipboard, plywood, block-board, Multiple Density Fibre Board (MDF), hardboard, veneer, solid or soft wood. It is interesting to note that some builders and carpenters refer to woods as "timber", while Americans call it "lumber". Polishers, however, still refer to it as "wood" – and why not? Before the final finish can be applied, the surface of the substrate has first to be prepared so as to produce a faultless finish with shellac, varnish, cellulose, wax etc., and the purpose of the preparation is to eradicate by hand or machine any fault on the surface of the substrate so that it will not be seen or noticed when the surface is finished.

The tools used in the preparation of a substrate are simple and consist basically of: a cabinet scraper, abrasive papers, a sanding block, an old screw driver or file, power sanding tools (orbital or belt sanding machines), and a dusting brush.

Before starting work on a substrate it is best to make a check list: Look at the substrate from various light-reflecting angles. Touch or feel the surface and look for any of the following faults and then decide on the method of eradication.

1. Scratches along or across the grain.
2. Bruises on the surface.
3. Splits or shakes.
4. Knots.
5. Woodworm flight holes (during restoration work).
6. Woodworking machine markings.
7. Chipboard bruises on the surface or on corners.
8. Holes or dents.

Resin bond filler applied to a sapele substrate. Using hessian to apply the woodfiller applied to open grain, rubbing in across the grain

Wiping off surplus filler across the grain

Oil bound filler applied to mahogany substrate

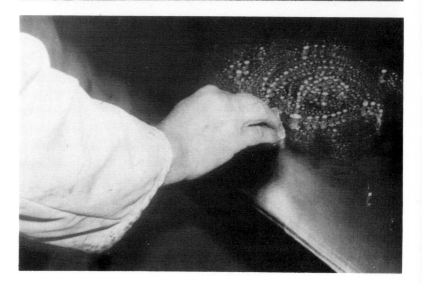

9. Veneers lifting or blisters.
10. Joint cavities in plywood or blockboard.

Furniture in bare new wood to be finished in a natural colour (no stain) is sometimes called "in the white". Restored substrates demand the same attention as new wood – sometimes more in fact – such as the eradication of ink or rust stains.

The eradication process during the preparation in wood

Scratches

If the substrate is solid wood, then there is no problem – simply scrape out the scratch using a sharp cabinet scraper and finish off with 100/240 grades of garnet papers used in conjunction with a cork block. If the wood is veneered, however, great caution is required as veneers will not stand up to cabinet scraping. A good guideline here is that the older the furniture, the thicker the veneers will be, but modern furniture veneers are extremely thin and these can easily be sanded down to the bare wood. Once the veneer has been sanded through, the substrate is useless unless great skill, time and effort are expended in fitting new veneer sections.

Scratches can be removed by simply sanding. On bare wood, scratches can be eradicated by applying water by pencil brush to the scratch cavity to raise the grain within the scratch area. It is then allowed to dry; the area treated with water will have swollen up and can be sanded flat.

Bruises

These can be steamed out by using an old screwdriver or file – the tips being heated over a flame and simply pressed down over a damp cloth over the bruise area, thus swelling the fibres of the wood to come up to the level of the surrounding wood surface. When dry, sand down using 240 grade garnet papers, to a smooth surface finish.

Splits or shakes

These tend to be natural faults found in wood and can be dealt with by using what is called a "stopper". These can be:
1. *A paste of fast-drying properties.* Comes in various colours such as pine, mahogany, oak, teak etc., in pre-packed tins, ready for use. The paste is pressed into the split and allowed to dry, then sanded flat using 240 grade garnet papers.
2. *Shellac sticks.* These are coloured hard shellac like sealing wax and require heating with a hot iron. The wax melts and is dropped into the cavity where it dries instantly. These shellac stick stoppers have a

Top of antique desk with multiple blisters.
Preparation work prior to re-finishing

Cutting at base of blister and applying glue
inside cavity

Pressing down using masking tape to keep
veneer in position until dry

nasty habit of becoming loose and falling out of the cavities, but are still useful.

3. *Beaumontage.* A modern formula has been developed recently using the traditional "beaumontage" – that is variously coloured sealing waxes containing beeswax resins. It has the advantage of being used without melting.

4. *Carnauba wax, Beeswax or Japan wax.* These are also ideal for small holes, splits or shakes. Carnauba wax requires melting like shellac sticks, while beeswax and Japan waxes can simply be applied by pressing a small piece of the wax into the cavity and sanding flat.

5. *Sawdust jam.* This stopper is made by mixing sawdust of the substrate with a little PVA or animal glue, and pressing it into the cavity. When dry it can be sanded down flat.

Knots

These can create a problem for the wood finisher – with pine in particular. No matter how the substrate is prepared and finished the knots will "show up" or protrude above the surrounding surface area or ooze out resin. The best way to deal with them is by sanding down really flat and filling the cracks around the knot with a stopper. If the final finish of the substrate is to be varnish or paint then two coats of a "knotting shellac" – generally a dewaxed shellac – should be applied over the knot. This will do two important things: firstly it will seal in the resin in the knot and, secondly, fill in the cracks around the knot which together will prevent the knot "bleeding", and spoiling the varnish or paint. The bleeding is due to the varnish or paint lying on a resinous area thus preventing the knot area from drying out naturally as it would if left untreated.

Woodworm flight holes

These must first be treated with a reliable woodworm fluid, to eradicate the woodworms or grubs, and allowed to dry out. The flight holes can be filled with any coloured patent stopper and sanded flat.

Wood-working machine markings

These are ugly bruises – slight burn marks – caused by the block planer or band saw which can also leave irregular cutting marks. These faults require eradication either by the smoothing plane or by sanding with abrasive papers – aluminium oxide papers are ideal for this process followed by garnet papers. The aluminium oxide papers used either by hand or power have greater cutting or biting action than others and on woods such as oak, walnut etc. are ideal, but it they are being used on a power orbital sanding machine then great care is required or unsightly marks can still be left on the surface. Belt sanders are far superior for this work, but should never be used on veneered substrates.

Veneered chipboard bruises

These can be troublesome in preparation and there are two ways of overcoming the problem. First, use the hot iron and damp rag method. If this is not acceptable, simply cut around the bruises and press a stopper made of sawdust and glue into the cavity using a wooden toothpick. Press it down flat, sticking a piece of masking tape over the area. When dry, remove the tape and sand flat. This method will not interrupt the continuity of the veneer flow on the surface.

Holes and dents

These are filled by using any of the stoppers mentioned or by simply pressing filler into the cavities and sanding flat. On the slower-drying patent stopper it is best to leave a convex layer over the hole area as on drying it can otherwise become concave.

Veneers lifting

This is a difficult fault to deal with and should not be underestimated. First, lift a little of the veneer and force glue, either PVA or animal (scotch), beneath it using a tooth-pick, and then press or roll it down flat and stick the area down with masking tape. A slight hammering pressure can be used with care on the edges. On veneer "bubbles", blisters or raised sections, *do not* on any account cut across the blistered area – simply cut around one side of the blister and with a tooth-pick force glue into the cavity and press down flat or use a roller. A veneer hammer is not much use here as it can cause more damage or tear up the blister. The use of a hot iron on a damp rag or silver foil is occasionally of some help, but the glue method is far superior and positive. Once the blister is glued down, apply two pieces of masking tape cross ways, roll down again and leave to dry out and harden, then simply remove the tape and sand down flat using 240 grade garnet abrasive papers.

Joints in veneer-surfaced boards

These are problems which can be unsightly if not eradicated. Simply use a stopper to fill the cavities between the joinings of the veneers – either a patent stopper or a sawdust jam and sand down flat when dry.

Traditional finishing, such as french polish, has always emphasised that the grain of the wood be filled so that the finish is a perfect gloss surface. Thank goodness that times have changed! For generations furniture and pianos have been finished to resemble glass and thus hiding the very texture of the wood. Since the introduction of spray gun modern finishes, open grain finishes have proved extremely popular with manufacturers of furniture, pianos and organs. Today with the advent of cellulose and synthetic lacquer, the full beauty of a piece of wood can be enhanced with a full gloss lacquer and yet still remain looking like wood and not a piece of plastic.

Sealers

These are in fluid form, and are also called sanding sealers. The purpose of a sealer is to "seal" the rough fibres of the wood surface and "harden up" the surface of the wood skin. It can also be used as a "sealing in skin" to fix stain colour. Sealers in fluid form sprayed or mopped on can sometimes be better than woodfillers on such fine-grained woods as beech or mahogany type woods. Shellac dewaxed sealers are used to apply over a very absorbent surface and also to seal as a buffer coat between troublesome woods, such as rosewood and teak, to form a barrier between cellulose finishes and these woods. Some sealers can be used to fad or mop on a thick film to take the place of "bodying in" in the french polishing process to save time.

There are three basic types of sealers:

1. Shellac dewaxed sanding sealers (milk-coloured). These are compatible with all traditional finishes such as french polish, varnish or wax. They consist of dewaxed shellac with IM spirits and can either be "white" or brownish in colour.
2. Cellulose-based sanding and base coating sealers which are compatible with modern cellulose or nitrocellulose materials. These consist of zinc or aluminium stearates with cellulose thinners. They are a slightly milky colour which dries clear.
3. Special sealers compatible with pre-catalysed, polyurethane, polyester or other synthetic finishing materials. These sealers do not contain stearates and no other sealer should be used under these lacquers or the resultant surface coatings will break up, due to the chemical reaction resulting from incompatibility.

Sealers can be applied by: mop, spray gun at 45-50 PSI pressure, fad, or dipping.

They must be left to dry for at least four hours or more before flatting by abrasive paper can take place, even though they may seem to be dry well within the time. A much improved surface finish can ultimately be achieved by using if at all possible a sealer. In recent years many sealers and filling products have "slid" onto the market, especially for the DIY trade. The only draw-back is choosing the correct product – a far cry from when polishers only had plaster of paris to fill or seal wood grain.

STAINING WOOD

Pass any furniture or piano showroom and look closely at the multitude of different "colours" produced by manufacturers and I am sure you will understand the complexity of colouring wood. I am not at the moment discussing finishes such as french polish, varnish or lacquers, but simply the colouring matter before finishing takes place, and why and how it is used on wood.

What makes woodworkers, when they have produced anything from a coffee table to a flight of stairs want to colour the wood? Any one of the various types of dyeing or staining agents can be used for any of the following reasons:

1. To give the wood an artistic or decorative appearance.
2. To show up or emphasize the graining and figuring in the wood. A figure is a term usually used to describe wood which possesses unusual or attractive natural designs in texture and natural colour in the form of "ribbons" or "burls" caused by skilled cutting of the log in the sawmills, or in veneer cutting.
3. To match new woods or veneers to old, or to blend different woods, when for instance repairing furniture or restoring antiques.
4. To make inferior woods such as pine resemble, for instance, walnut – a common practice now in the furniture trade.
5. Tradition – the colouring of wood has been practised for thousands of years. The ancient Egyptians covered their furniture in heavy coloured shellac and gold leaf, as relics in their excavated tombs reveals.
6. To preserve the wood – most external preservatives have colouring matter in them as well as preserving salts and chemicals. Various well-known manufacturers have trade brands of external wood fluid preservatives to provide a range of colours including red cedar for roof shingles, dark oak for floor boards and transparent green for greenhouses. The faithful creosote, derived from coal-tar is also now available in light, golden and dark shades for all external softwoods – for fencing, telegraph poles etc.
7. To blend in woods to suit surrounding existing furniture – no use having a piece of mahogany furniture or joinery in a room full of tudor furniture – the new must therefore blend in with the existing colour of dark oak in this example.

Colouring wood is an exciting adventure for both the DIY amateur and the skilled professional. The wonderful effects that various fluids can create is inexhaustible in skilled hands, but in order to utilize them to the full it is necessary to know something about the basic rules of colour. Colour is just as vital to furniture as the finish – more so in fact – if the colour is wrong then the finish suffers.

There are three primary colours – red, blue and yellow – so called because they are natural colours and cannot be produced by combining any other colours together, and there are secondary colours which are produced by combining together two or more of the primary colours as shown by the table:

Yellow + Red = Orange
Blue + Red = Purple
Blue + Yellow = Green

In nature, white is a combination of all colours, as in light, and black is the total absence of colour as in full darkness, but these "colours" have been reproduced and to add to the table therefore:–

Black + White = Grey

Tints are primary or secondary colours with the addition of white. Shades are primary or secondary colours with the addition of black. Tones are primary or secondary colours with the addition of grey. The endless variety of "browns" which are used to colour woods are produced from a combination of the three primary colours with black and white in various proportions. Many of these colours are to be found in natural occurring "earth" substances, but most other colours can be chemically reproduced.

Wood colours fall into two main categories – pigments and dyes or stains.

Pigments

These are used when obliteration or partial obliteration of the wood is required, and consist basically of natural mineral pigments. Earth pigments have been with us for hundreds of years but were developed and made famous by the great Italian "renaissance" painters – such pigments as burnt umber, venetian red, burnt sienna, yellow ochre, titanium white, brunswick green, ultramarine blue, orange chrome and lamp black. Nowadays, however, most pigments are chemically produced and their production is very complex. The demand for exciting new colours has produced shades of purple, green, red, blue for colouring furniture. Due to the development of the spray gun and spray application, wood finishers are now out of the rut of simply finishing in the basic walnut, mahogany and oak traditional colours. I have seen grand pianos finished in green with the grain showing another colour – white, the whole effect splatter finished with gold and red speckles and finished with matt lacquer. I must say it is very refreshing to see this type of new approach to colouring furniture.

Pigments are most frequently used either for application by spray-gun or for "touching-in", and are best mixed with methylated spirits and a little de-waxed shellac sealer as a binder, and applied either with the spray-gun or with a mop or "touch-up" pencil brush which must be

used with great care and skill. A point to bear in mind however is that pigments mixed in this way do not penetrate the grain but merely lie on top of the surface like paint. They tend not to be very lightfast, but are nevertheless excellent for "touching-in" or for "tea-wash" spray coatings over stained surfaces to blend in a colour. The above mixture is used for traditional finishes, but pigments can also be used in conjunction with lacquers, and if mixed with a little lacquer and thinners can be used on cellulose and synthetic coatings for "touching-in". It must be noted that some pigments are spirit-based and are to be mixed with spirit; and some are water-based which are to be mixed with water, so it is important to make the correct choice.

Dyes and stains

A dye or stain, which is produced from aniline and coal-tar sources is intended to colour the wood without obliterating the grain in any way, unlike pigments. It does this by penetrating the fibres of the wood, and as different fibres absorb varying amounts of the fluid colour depending on the chemical make-up of the wood, this can have the effect of enhancing the beauty of attractive figuring or graining. A knot in pine for instance will absorb very little or no stain, but a section of end-grain or cross-planed sections of wood will drink up a large amount of stain. Stains or dyes are soluble in either spirit, water, naphtha or oil. They must be colour-fast, have minimum chemical reactivity with any surface coating, and not run or bleed easily once a finishing coat is applied.

Those available on the market today consist basically of:
1. Oil stains – available from most DIY shops, stores and trade houses.
2. Spirit stains from artists' shops and trade houses.
3. Chemical stains from various sources such as chemists and trade houses.
4. Water stains from trade houses.
5. Varnish stains and naphtha stains from DIY shops, stores and trade houses.
6. Preservatives with added colours for external use only – obtainable from ironmongers, builders merchants, garden centres etc.

The subject of staining wood is a complex one, and of great importance to the wood-finisher. No matter how good the joinery or cabinet-making, the finish is what is noticed and it can make or mar the finished piece of work.

Oil stains or dyes

These are the most common types of staining material available on the DIY market today. They are supplied in quantities from 250 ml. to 5 litres, ready for use. The colours available include English oak, dark Jacobean, dark oak, Spanish mahogany, mahogany, walnut, teak, light oak, cedar and medium oak. This range is oil-based (turpentine substitute) or synthetic solvent-based, and with a small amount of binder to hold the colour have drying times between 3-8 hours according to temperature in the drying area, which should not be lower than 65°F. These stains can be used on new soft wood, restored surfaces, plywood, chipboard, blockboard, MDF board, veneers and hardboard and will sink deeply into the surface and enhance the beauty of the grain. Most oil stains tend to fade but the modern range of stains now available is lightfast.

Applying oil stains

1. Empty the contents from the manufacturer's tin into a broad open-necked tin or jar.
2. Apply with a fad or lint-free linen cloth or a polisher's mop.
3. Apply in the direction of the grain only – never across the grain.
4. Apply as quickly as possible and avoid overlapping.
5. Apply one coat at a time and allow to try out thoroughly before applying the second.
6. Do not leave a lake of stain on the substrate, but wipe off any surplus with either a clean rag or absorbent paper.
7. Leave for 6-8 hours to dry out in a day warm place before applying a surface coating of any kind.

If you intend to use a finishing coat of varnish such as a polyurethane or cellulose lacquer, whether it be semi-glass or matt, a thin coating of bleached shellac should first be applied over the stain – not french polish as this contains wax. Allow it to dry, then slightly sand it down using 320 Lubrisil Silicon Carbide or 240 garnet abrasive paper. This

Applying an oil stain by rag

Removing surplus oil stain with a clean rag in the direction of grain

will prevent "bleeding" when the surface coating of varnish or cellulose is applied.

Advantages of oil stains

1. They can be purchased ready for use in 125 ml., 250 ml., 500 ml. and 2.5 litre or 5 litre tins or containers.
2. Consistent colour charts are available and those in the same product range can be intermixed, although it is not advisable to mix stains from different manufacturers together.
3. They can be ordered repeatedly without fear of any colour variation.

4. They are simple to use and can be applied by brush, mop or fad.
5. They have very good penetrating qualities.
6. When dry they leave the grain clear and unobliterated.
7. They artistically improve the graining effect.
8. They do not raise the grain of the wood.
9. The stain is reversible by the use of oil solvents such as white spirit and can therefore be easily stripped off if required.
10. They are ideal for covering very large surfaces such as wall panels, doors etc.
11. They are – in some cases depending on the manufacturer – lightfast or resistant to fading.

Disadvantages of oil stains

1. The basic shades available are limited to "timber" colours i.e. oaks, mahoganies etc.
2. Drying times are slow – at least 6-8 hours before a second or further coat can be applied.
3. Lacquers or varnishes or waxes will make the stain bleed if applied directly over it.
4. Stains react differently on certain woods – for instance, if a rosewood colour is applied to mahogany it will darken it, but if applied to pine a patchy, greasy red/brown effect is produced. Areas around knots will absorb very little or no stain at all, showing up light. End grain will drink up large amounts, thus showing up dark.
5. They can be somewhat expensive.
6. They are not suitable for use under a surface coating of pre-catalysed or acid-catalysed lacquer where a completely heat and stain/water resisting finish is required and therefore tend to reduce the advantages of the lacquers.
7. If two or more coatings or oil stains are used on the same substrate, a deposit is left on the surface of the wood which must be removed by a dry cloth. A greater length of drying time is therefore required for each coating of the stain which could lead to two or three days duration.
8. If glues have been used on the substrate at any time, oil stains will simply not penetrate these areas, and ugly sections are left for extra attention by "touching-in" with pigmented colours.

Spirit stains

These stains are made up from dyes such as aniline, or from pigments, using methylated spirits as a solvent with a little bleached shellac as a binder, and the aniline dye or pigment must therefore be soluble in spirit. This cuts down the range of colours, as not all aniline dyes are spirit soluble. Dyes for spirit stains include Bismark brown, Chrysoidine (red), purple and greens, while for pigments, brown umber, yellow ochre, burnt sienna, orange chrome, black oxide – to name a few – are the important colours.

These types of stains have limitations as they are used mainly to obliterate the grain. They are made as strong as possible simply by adding more of the powder colour, whether it be aniline or pigment, to the medium which is spirit plus shellac or for very thin washes they use very little of the colours. I describe this as a "tea-wash".

A grand piano pedal unit of rosewood stained with a spirit stain to restore the colour

Applying spirit stains

1. Drying is rapid due to the evaporation of the spirit, and they must therefore be applied with speed and skill. A typical mixture of a spirit stain would be 80% methylated spirits, 10% shellac sealer and 10% pigment, used just as a stain. If used for touching-in purposes then the proportions would be 50% methylated spirits, 10% shellac sealer and 40% pigment.
2. Apply with a mop, brush, rag or spray gun.
3. Apply in the direction of the grain – never across it.
4. Avoid overlapping as this will cause streaks or darker shades where overlapping has taken place.

Advantages of spirit stains

1. Very fast drying time by evaporation of the spirit – 2-10 minutes.
2. Very strong colours which can be intermixed for obliteration of the grain.
3. Can be sprayed on as a "tea-wash" – a very thin fluid – to blend in a colour. Either methylated spirits with a shellac or cellulose thinners with a little neat cellulose can be used.
4. Excellent in the "touching-up" technique – that is applying these stains by pencil brush for highlights and colouring over faults in wood.
5. Can be used for simulating grain effects.
6. Will not raise the grain of the wood.
7. Ideal for use under cellulose lacquers.
8. Ideal for splatter colouring by spray gun.

Disadvantages of spirit stains

1. They are not lightfast and tend to fade.
2. They have poor penetration and tend to "float" within the spirit medium on top of a surface, and if the surface coating is scratched deep the wood will show through white, unlike other stains.
3. It is difficult to cover large areas due to the very speedy drying times, and is impossible to avoid overlapping.
4. They can obliterate the grain.
5. There is a limited colour range.
6. They dry far too quickly.
7. They are not pre-packed nor colour-controlled like oil stains so there is no continuity in colour blending. You simply mix your own colour using your own skill and knowledge.

Chemical stains

The exciting thing about applying a chemical stain is in watching the fantastic change on a piece of wood happen so dramatically before your eyes. It is normally a colourless fluid – with the exception of say permanganate of potash and bichromate of potash. This is why it is unlike other forms of staining, when you know what "colour" you are applying. You do not know with a chemical stain – you wait for the outcome.

These stains are mostly used by professional wood finishers, antique restorers, quality joiners and furniture manufacturers. The colours produced by chemical reaction on woods are permanent because they react with the natural chemicals contained in the various fibres, such as tannic acid, which is endemic in oak for example. Not all wood, however, contains sufficient tannic acid to produce the effects required.

Health and safety warning

Anyone trying out these chemical stains for the first time must realise that most of the chemicals which are mentioned in this chapter are dangerous to the skin; and toxic, so protective clothing – gloves, eye goggles etc. must be worn. Normal workshop hygiene should also be followed both before and after use, such as using protective hand creams and washing the hands carefully. One point to remember is that you must always add acids to water slowly to dilute them – never the other way round or you could have a shower explosion in your face. This also applies to alkaline solutions such as caustic soda (called lye in America), when the water will boil when the chemical is added. Remember too that both acid and alkaline solutions must be stored in properly labelled glass containers.

The chemicals

When applied to wood, these cause a reaction to take place within the natural chemical structure of the fibres of the wood, producing a change of colour. Most chemicals used by the wood-finisher for staining can be found in the ordinary household cupboard, either in the kitchen or the garden shed, and can be obtained from the local chemist, hardware store or grocer. They are mainly used by restorers of antiques or in other situations where mature colouring is required, for example when making repairs to church furniture which is to blend in with the old colour. These stains are mainly used by professional polishers, but there is no reason why a skilled amateur should not be able to use them with fascinating results.

Chemical stains fall into two groups – alkalis and acids, both of which are water based. Alkalis consist of a series of compounds called bases which are highly soluble in water and produce a caustic or corrosive solution. An acid is a substance composed of hydrogen and other elements and is corrosive.

I give below a list of both the acid and alkaline chemical stains in common use today:
1. Bichromate or dichromate of potash.
2. Copper sulphate, known as blue copperas.

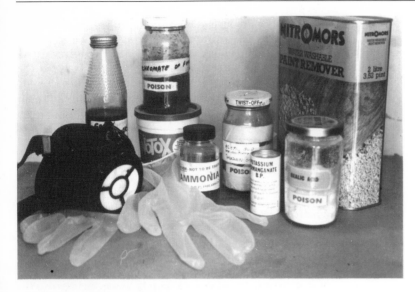

Chemicals in popular use, with gloves and face mask

3. Ferrous sulphate, known as green copperas.
4. Nitric acid.
5. Sulphric acid.
6. Permanganate of potash.
7. Acetic acid (weak vinegar).
8. Ammonia (.880 strength – very strong).
9. Tannic acid.
10. Pyrogallic acid.

Not every wood is affected by chemical staining. Teak, cedar, rose-wood and ebony, to name but a few, are useless for chemical staining due to their strong natural chemical structure. Here are more details of some of the effects you can expect from these stains:

1. Bichromate or dichromate of potash is available in the form of yellow/orange/red crystals (toxic) and a concentrated solution is made by steeping the crystals in warm water (use rain or distilled water as water in certain areas is too hard). The stain when mixed reacts with the tannic acid found in some wood such as oak and chestnut and quickly darkens the wood within five minutes. Mahogany is also affected by this stain and darkens. It is to be noted that to obtain a more even staining effect, the wood can be pre-treated with tannic acid (or very strong tea), and allowed to dry, and then coated with this stain which will then ensure that a more positive colouring takes place. Any wood which does not contain tannic acid can be treated in this way.

2. Copper sulphate, which is known as blue copperas, is toxic when dissolved in water, and will colour some woods a bluish dark grey.

3. Ferrous sulphate, or sulphate of iron, is known as green copperas or even green vitriol and is also toxic. This stain reacts on some woods to produce a silvery grey colour, the iron salts acting on the tannic acid contained in the cells of the wood. The principal use of green copperas is to colour-tone oak to silvery grey and also to reduce redness in mahogany.

4. Nitric acid requires great care in use and should not be attempted by the novice. It is a colourless, highly corrosive liquid which, when diluted in a 4-1 proportion with water produces a yellowish tone. Undiluted it produces a red/brown/yellow stain on certain woods.
5. Sulphuric acid used in full strength produces a light brown colour on oak, light and dark green on pine. It is also used diluted in the acid finish with french polishing.
6. Permanganate of potash consists of common violet crystals, which, when used in the proportion of 2 oz. to 2 pints of soft rain water darkens oak and ash to brown tones. It reacts quickly but tends to fade in time.
7. Mild acetic acid or white vinegar, when combined with iron filings which have been soaked for eight hours and then strained off, will colour pine or oak a weathered dark grey or even black depending on the strength. It is quick-acting, 2-10 minutes depending on strength, and is ideal for antique distressing because it is permanent.
8. Ammonia used in the normal trade strength of .880 or 35% pure ammonia which is very concentrated, will darken oak slightly. As a comparison household ammonia is about 5% strength! Used in the 'fumed' state, it will darken oak and mahogany fairly quickly, say 3-6 hours duration.
9. Tannic acid. Oak contains tannic acid, and it is this which reacts with the ammonia in the fuming technique. Before synthetic chemicals were developed, oak bark was steeped in water as one of the only sources of tannic acid. If iron nails are used in oak, these will also react and produce a black colour. Tannic acid in a milder form is also to be found in strong cold tea after the leaves have been steeped for an hour or so.
10. Pyrogallic acid, which is an extract from gallnuts, is used to coat woods prior to fuming and will give a richer, redder tone than tannic acid. It can be mixed with tannic acid to give a slightly half-way tone of a brown/red colour by the fuming process.

Other examples of chemical stains on wood are *alkaline solutions* such as *caustic soda* or *lye* which reacts on pine and darkens it. We all know that strong, hot caustic soda also strips wood, but I am only concerned here with the staining properties of these chemicals. *Washing soda* will darken some woods to a yellowish brown, while *slaked lime* has a weathering effect on oak. Equal parts of caustic soda and lime in water produce a "pickled pine" effect.

Applying chemical stains

Apply with a rag, fad or sponge and then allow to dry out thoroughly. The following points should be remembered when using chemical stains:
1. Always wear protective clothing, including gloves and eye goggles, when handling.
2. Keep good ventilation in the work area.
3. When diluting acids, these must be added to water – never the other way round.

4. Alkalis and acids must be stored in a cool place in glass containers and properly labelled.
5. When dry, other orthodox stains such as oil or spirit stains can be applied over them.
6. The colouring qualities of these chemicals cannot be precisely predicted, but, once applied THEY ARE NOT REVERSIBLE, and therefore it is advisable to
(i) always mix sufficient for any work project in one batch
(ii) always try out the stain on an off-cut of the timber you are using before applying it to the finished piece, or, in the case of an existing piece, in some hidden place.
7. Give 12-24 hours drying time before finishing the surface coating.
8. It is not advisable to use chemical stains on such woods as teak, rosewood or cedar, as these woods have complex natural chemical structures within themselves and no advantage would result in using chemical stains.
9. Some alkaline solutions other than ammonia which produce dark colours on wood tend to leave a "salt" residue of alkali on the surface of the wood which must be washed off clean with a neutralizing coat of mild acetic acid (vinegar) and allowed to dry before proceeding with oil, wax or shellac finishing.
10. Strong acetic acid of more than 20% strength is very dangerous to use and great care should be taken in handling it – you could loose the skin from your fingers so wear rubber or plastic gloves and guard against splashing any other exposed areas of skin.

Chemical fuming using .880 ammonia

Fuming is a darkening process. It was very popular during the period 1890-1930, and was mainly used to darken furniture. Today it is only used by the craftsman on restoration work to achieve this darkening tone on basically English and Baltic oaks. Chestnut, rich in tannic acid, reacts with fuming, while mahogany and walnut turn to a brown tone.

Procedure for fuming

The operation of a fumigation chamber is simple. Construct a "tent" of transparent polythene and place the work piece inside the tent – for example an oak table – after first removing all brasswork otherwise this will also be affected. Place half a dozen small saucers filled with .880 ammonia around the work piece before sealing up the tent with sealing tape. After a few hours the oak will darken, the reason being that the ammonia fumes have reacted with the tannic acid in the oak. The grain is not raised. The process can be speeded up by coating the wood with tannic acid in the proportion of 1 oz. to 1 qt. of water. Pyrogallic acid can be used instead of tannic acid in the proportion of ¾ oz. to 1 qt. water to produce a redder tone. Not all woods contain tannic acid, but beech, for example, if first coated with tannic acid before being placed in the fumigation chamber will darken like the oaks. Teak is not suitable for fuming. Pre-coated surfaces give a more even colour than un-treated woods when fumed. One great advantage in fuming is that no liquid touches the wood, so the grain is not raised.

When fuming has been completed, the surface can then be finished with wax polish, oil finish or shellac etc.

Advantages of chemical stains

1. They can penetrate deep into the fibres of wood better than other stains.
2. If used warm they penetrate even deeper.
3. Colours produced on wood are permanent.
4. Water is the basic solvent, therefore the stains are cheaper than oil or spirit stains.
5. Depth of shade can be adjusted by adding more or less solvent (water).
6. Chemical stains are mainly purchased in dry form – powder or crystal.
7. Mainly used in the antique restoring trade and on good quality joinery.
8. One or more chemicals can be coated onto the wood provided that each chemical is allowed to dry out before applying other chemicals on top. The results are due to the reaction of the various chemicals on each other and on the wood.

Disadvantages of chemical stains

1. As they are water-based, they tend to raise the grain.
2. Drying times are long – approximately 24 hours.
3. Great care is required in handling many of them and protective clothing, barrier creams and gloves and goggles should be used.
4. They are not available "pre-packed" as are oil and water stains.

Water stains

These are the most important stains. They were mainly used by professional wood finishers and furniture manufacturers, but they are now becoming increasingly popular in the DIY trade. The dyes used in water stains are from aniline and coal tar sources but are not entirely new as the first coal tar dye was produced as far back as 1865.

One trade brand of water stains on the market is produced in a twelve colour shade range – light oak, middle oak, black oak, grey oak, teak, brown mahogany, red mahogany, rich brown walnut, rosewood, golden oak, dark oak, and moss green. As all colours can be inter-mixed, virtually any shade can be produced. These are long lasting stains which penetrate the grain and enhance the wood because they give a transparent colour without obliterating the grain or mudding the colour. Water stains, when dry can be finished with any surface coating such as varnish, nitrocellulose, pre-catalysed lacquers, french polish, oil or wax.

Applying water stains

They should be applied by rag, fad or sponge with the direction of the grain and as quickly as possible without overlapping.

Advantages of water stains

1. Any colour or shade can be produced for matching.
2. They are obtainable in pre-packaged tins or as powders.
3. They will not fade in strong sunlight or weathering.
4. They give a clear transparent colour to wood.
5. They do not obliterate the grain.
6. They are reasonably inexpensive.
7. They are compatible with any surface coating.
8. They do not leave a muddy surface on drying.
9. They are ideal for traditional and modern cellulose surface coatings because there is no chemical interaction.

Disadvantages of water stains

1. The solvent is water which raises the grain causing rough surfaces. To avoid this the wood should be pre-wetted and allowed to dry, and then sanded down with garnet papers before the application of water stains.
2. They cannot be used on veneers which have a water-based glue. The veneers may swell.
3. Skill is required in application to avoid streaks and overlaps.
4. On certain woods such as teak, ebony and cedar they have poor penetration.
5. At least twelve hours drying time must be allowed depending on temperature, for the substrate to dry.
6. They should not be used on surfaces that have been chemically stripped due to their poor penetration of these surfaces.

Useful tips on water stains

1. Van Dyke Brown crystals mixed with water as the solvent is a traditional basic standard water stain for walnut shades – and a little added ammonia or detergent will help the stain to penetrate deeper into the fibres of the wood. These must not be used under cellulose or pre-catalysed lacquers.
2. Rain water is better than tap water for mixing water stains, especially if you live in a very hard water area, such as London or Gloucestershire.

3. The surface must be bone dry before any surface coating can be applied.

In recent years there has been renewed interest in water stains, the factors such as drying times, grain raising and penetration are being improved and further developed.

Varnish stains

This is a method of applying both a colour and a surface coating to wood in one operation. These varnish stains will greatly improve pale and uninteresting woods and make them look much more attractive simply by applying the coloured varnish straight from the tin using a good varnish brush. It is advisable to apply one coat of the varnish stain and allow it to dry for approximately 72 hours. Sand this down with Lubrisil 320 grade silicon carbide paper, dust down with a "Tak" rag to absorb dust etc., and finally apply one or two coats of polyurethane gloss, semi-gloss (satin) or matt varnish, whichever is preferred.

Most varnish companies have stained varnish wood shades of light oak, medium oak, dark oak, deep red mahogany, Jacobean oak, sapele shade, dark Jacobean, dark mahogany, walnut and teak which is available in 125 ml, 250 ml, 500 ml, 1 litre or 5 litre tins.

Advantages of varnish stains

1. They are very easy to apply – straight from the tin using a brush.
2. Very little skill is required in application, so they are ideal for the amateur who can obtain fairly good results from these products.
3. A good choice of colours is available from most manufacturers.
4. They have a reasonable drying time – between six and twelve hours.
5. They will not fade.
6. They are ideal for inexpensive furniture and joinery work.
7. They are easily available from DIY, hardware or ironmongery shops.

Disadvantages of varnish stains

1. They have very poor penetration qualities.
2. They are not recommended for antique furniture or high class work.
3. The surface finish shows a heavy build-up of varnish.
4. They have a tendency to obliterate the grain.
5. They require good ventilation during application, particularly the polyurethane type. Some may contain isocyanates which could give anyone not using a mask or good ventilation a bad headache for several days.

Naphtha stains

These are penetrating wood stains produced mainly for the professional trade. They give a transparent colour to the wood which is free from muddiness and reasonably lightfast. They are easy to apply by either rag or fad and dry very quickly. Special naphtha thinners must be used – white spirit and distillates are *not* recommended for use with this type of stain. Normal traditional wood-colouring shades are produced by various manufacturers.

Advantages of naphtha stains

1. They have very rapid drying times, bone dry within one hour, so work can progress more quickly.
2. They do not show a green fluorescence under cellulose as some other stains do.
3. They are obtained in batch-controlled, ready-to-use fluids in containers.
4. They are ideal for a mass-production line.

Disadvantages of naphtha stains

1. They are expensive.
2. They are not recommended for spraying, or for shading, touching-in, colouring etc.
3. Special thinners must be used as a solvent.
4. Skill is required in application due to the rapid drying and extreme penetration in order to avoid overlapping.

Wood preserving stains

These are not basically stains in themselves, but oils containing various active chemical ingredients such as copper or zinc as naphthenate. Sometimes they have added colouring matter.

Two major manufacturers of these products in this country provide a range of preservative fluids with added colouring matter – for instance "Red Cedar" which is specially formulated to protect and recolour weathered cedar when used for roof shingles, cladding, greenhouses etc. Other colours produced are dark oak, light oak, green and clear, which contains no added colour, and is for use where preservation is required without alteration of colour. The oaks are ideal for such projects as treating large floor-board areas and interior beams as well as external woodwork, whereas the green is mainly for greenhouses, seed-boxes, joists and roof rafters. Most of these preservative stains have a fairly low odour and soon dry to a satin sheen. They are now coming onto the home market "water-based" external wood preservatives with silicones that are stated to last longer than the more orthodox oil-based preservatives, but time will prove whether this is so or not.

Application of preserving stains

Mainly by brush, but spray equipment can be used in cases where access is difficult.

Advantages of wood preserving stains

1. They are cheaper than paint surface coatings.
2. They are water resisting.
3. They prevent rot and insect attack.
4. They have a low odour.
5. They dry rapidly.
6. They are colourfast.
7. They are harmless to plant life.

Disadvantages of wood preserving stains

1. Care must be taken to provide adequate ventilation when they are used for interior timberwork.
2. Suitable protective clothing must be worn, such as gloves, plus a hand barrier cream to prevent skin troubles or discoloration, and a face mask when in a confined space.
3. Most of these fluids have fumes which are harmful to fish, and animals and children should be kept away from treated areas until the fumes have dissipated.

A few tips of wood preserving stains

1. When treating a whole floor area, cover with polythene sheeting when application is complete and this will prevent fumes contaminating the whole house.
2. Use a good quality paintbrush for application.
3. Wipe off any spillages onto paintwork immediately with white spirit.
4. Do not smoke, drink or eat when using these fluids.
5. Always apply to external surfaces while the wood is bone dry and grain open – a hot dry day is ideal.

Non-grain raising stains

These are known as NGR stains – an American development not too popular in Britain. They are mixed solvent stains and the dyes used are the water-soluble acid types. The main solvent is one of the glycol ethers, and they are mostly used by large concerns on production lines etc.

Advantages of NGR stains

1. When applying wood fillers after staining, these have no effect on "lifting the colour" as oil stains do.
2. They are lightfast and will not fade.
3. They do not raise the grain at all.
4. They are fast in drying.
5. They are supplied in "packaged" form ready for use.
6. They have excellent penetrating qualities.
7. They can be sprayed on using a normal type of spray gun.

Disadvantages of NGR stains

1. They are expensive.
2. They penetrate too deeply into the fibres of wood, and this can cause blemishes.
3. They are not readily available to ordinary shoppers but are more or less restricted to the professional trade and industrial finishers.

SHELLAC

During a working day in any professional wood finisher's life, hardly an hour goes by when shellac is not used in some form or another. Shellac can be used as a french polish, a sealer, a binder, for fillers, a stopper when made into a "jam", as a spirit varnish or for use as a fixative for pigments. Shellac is as much the foundation to the wood finishing trade as bricks are to the building industry, yet it was man's first "do-it-yourself" material – in today's jargon a truly organic product.

It used to be known as "gum-lac" and has been used for many thousands of years for a variety of purposes. The Chinese became famous for dyeing silk and leather and it was also used to produce the deep red colour in carpets. The Egyptians, Greeks and Romans were also known for their use of this lac dye. Gum lac has been used as an adhesive for fixing precious stones into sword handles, to produce and decorate other items of jewellery, as a cosmetic by eastern women, and as a medicine thought to cure rheumatism and anaemia. The North American Indians are believed to have used it to prepare a protective finish for their bows and arrows and to decorate baskets and pottery. In more recent years, its use has been extended to insulation for electrical wiring, moulded articles (the first gramophone records were made of shellac), flexographic inks, the production of grinding wheels, and of course the most generally-known use in the manufacture of french polishes and "self-polishing" floor polishes and for the manufacture of shellac wax.

By the birth of the new era in world trade development in England in the early 17th century, "gum-lac" was being imported by our newly-founded import agents, The East India Company, though as yet only in small quantities. The western world became gradually more interested in this new red dye and gum extract from the East. The dye was used by the British Army for colouring their uniforms – the famous British Redcoat, although it is interesting to note that prior to the introduction of the gum-lac dye, the Army used the very expensive cochineal (another insect dye) from Mexico, but the lac dye was much cheaper. The trading in gum lac by The East India Company caused it to become one of India's major exports, and this coincided with the industrial expansion in Britain in the early 19th century.

In 1855, two men known as the "Angelo Brothers" opened the very

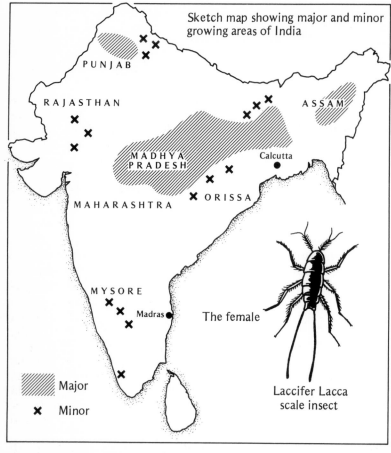

Sketch map showing major and minor growing areas of India

PUNJAB

RAJASTHAN

ASSAM

MADHYA PRADESH

Calcutta

MAHARASHTRA

ORISSA

MYSORE

Madras

The female

Laccifer Lacca
scale insect

▨ Major

✕ Minor

The cultivation of 'lac' (shellac)

first factory in Cossipore in India to produce and export lac dye to the western world. By 1870 its use had been extended and developed for the resin qualities, instead of the dye properties, in various industries, mainly due to the discovery of aniline dyes by Perkins's which were considerably cheaper than the gum-lac dyes. In 1872 the Angelo Brothers' factory commercially produced "Shellac" by using a new type of solvent process. Shellac is a refined form of lac with the word originally deriving from "shell-lac" – the thin flakes in which it is commonly marketed – although it is now used to cover all forms of refined lac.

The new solvent process coincided with the vast expansion in England and Europe of an entirely new way of finishing wood – known as "french polishing" which was ironically said to be doomed to failure by craftsmen of the era who believed it would not last – how wrong they are! Until the introduction of french polishing, all furniture, pianos and harpsichords were finished with beeswax and turpentine wax polish. Various enterprising manufacturers who made pianos and furniture introduced this new finish with great success. Within a few years it had replaced the slow, costly, labour-intensive process of wax finishing. "Broadwoods", the famous piano firm, who manufactured thousands of pianos each year, had as early as 1815 been the first to turn to the use of shellac in french polishing. Other firms followed their example so that french polish using shellac as the basic ingredient gradually became the major wood finishing product of the time, not only for pianos but for furniture and interior joinery used in offices, banks etc.

The demand grew for a steady supply of shellac. India was the main manufacturing and exporting centre to the UK, with many thousands of tons yearly. The development of "cellulose" wood finishes in the thirties and the later developments of acid catalyst cellulose products followed by polyester and polyurethane were taken up by manufacturers who wanted an even speedier, harder and heat and stain resistant surface coating with which to finish their products. In spite of this, shellac still survives in the hands of the traditional wood finisher and antique restorer.

Apart from India, shellac is produced in many parts of the world including Thailand, Southern China, Burma, Japan, Formosa, Africa, Sri Lanka and North America.

It is fascinating to note that the finishing trade throughout its history has depended on two insects for its basic raw materials – the bee and the Laccifer Lacca (Lac beetle). In both cases it is the female of the species which produces the beeswax and the lac. The lac insect has had in the past a number of names such as Coccus Lacca and Tachardia Lacca, but entomologists have given it the family group name of Laccifer Lacca. The male of the species is a bright red colour, but it is the female that is the producer of the lac. These insects are about one eighth of an inch in length fully grown and they attach themselves to the tender twigs or branches of such trees or bushes as the Palas, Ber or Kusum in India, and both the fig tree and the banana bush are also favourite hosts for these parasitic insects.

The larvae settle on the twigs in large numbers, around 100 to 150 per square inch, to feed from the sap juice. They quickly become covered with a layer of lac secreted from the glands under the skin of the insect, which is at first golden and then brownish. This gradually hardens and thickens as more lac is added from the inside. After about 6-8 weeks the larvae mature and there is a rapid increase in the lac secretion by the female insect which becomes purplish-red. It is this, plus the encrusted scales of the insects, which gives the lac its characteristic "sealing wax" appearance.

The encrusted twigs are called "stick-lac", which is composed of 70% lac resin, the other 30% being shellac, wax gluten and colouring matter.

Cultivation of the lac, or lac farming, is carried out by local people as a village industry on host trees on which two crops per year are obtained – in spring and autumn. The native cultivator either owns his own trees or rents them, and most practise a rotation system for harvesting the crop of stick lac. The spring crop is used mainly for propagation purposes, while the autumn crop is the main cash crop. In order to obtain a continuous supply, "ripe" Broodlac – encrusted stocks in which the larvae are developing – are bundled and tied to new host trees in order to infect them.

As well as enjoying the two lac crops, the cultivator, if he choses his host trees carefully enjoys the natural fruit of the host trees themselves. The "Ber" tree in India for example produces an edible plum, although the fruits of the fig and the banana are better known! To grow lac successfully the host trees must be fast growing and be able to recover rapidly from the heavy pruning that takes place during harvesting, for while dozens of varieties of trees throughout the world are suitable hosts for the laccifer lacca, only a few are practical for commercial cultivation. Different qualities of stick lac are produced in different areas.

Harvesting is done by cutting off the twigs which are then scraped or twisted to remove the encrustation and this is usually dried for several days before being marketed to the wholesaler.

The lac is at this stage full of impurities and is refined in the first instance, either in the village or the factory, by crushing, sieving, winnowing and washing out the dye to produce a semi-refined product called seedlac. This can be further refined and stretched into sheet which, when broken up become the familiar flaked shellac.

The wood finisher's use of shellac

Shellac flakes, when mixed with spirit, either denatured grain (ethyl) or wood (methyl) alcohol, dissolve. The product, when applied to wood dries out within minutes to a hard surface coating. This mixing process used to be carried out in glass containers but shellac is now stored in plastic containers. Mixed shellac can also be stored in metal containers but certain inhibitors have to be added to prevent corrosion and discoloration of the fluid in contact with the metal.

There is a degree of confusion about the difference between shellac and french polish. The latter is made up of shellac dissolved in methylated spirits, with additives such as gum arabic or gum copal and sometimes a little cellulose to make it slightly water resistant and to flow better. In the past, wood-finishers made their own french polish – and indeed some still do – usually by simply adding shellac flakes to methylated spirits, but nowadays the product is easily obtainable from most paint or hardware stores and trade houses. It comes in various forms:

Button Polish is an orange full-bodied polish ideal for most warm-coloured woods such as walnut, mahogany etc., while

Pale Polish or Extra Pale Polish which are really near-clear fluids are ideal for woods that are to be polished to allow the full beauty of the natural grain and colour of the wood to show through, so that elm for instance should be polished with pale polish and not button polish. The ever popular

White French Polish which looks like milk is ideal for such woods as pine as it inhibits discoloration, or for any wood that must have the natural finish, such as lime etc.

Garnet Polish is a dark-coloured polish and is ideal for all dark woods such as rosewood, mahogany, ebony etc. Garnet Polish is often referred to as AC Garnet – this is a polish dewaxed during the manufacturing process. Not only does the polish become dewaxed but it is decolorised by the process of Activated Carbonisation – hence AC

Garnet! Garnet polishes are ruby red or super blonded.

Coloured French Polish such as black (for piano finishes), and for the modern market, blues, reds, greens etc. can be made to order by various manufacturers.

Shellac Sealers have become popular during the past few years: these are generally bleached and dewaxed shellac products and make an ideal bodying surface undercoating.

Knotting is a dewaxed shellac product used for covering knots to prevent the sap causing damage to the surface coating which is sometimes called knot-weeping.

The advantages of shellac for the wood finisher are many. It can make an excellent sealer for the surface of wood in-the-white, and can be built up and flatted down between coats many times in the space of a few hours ready to take other finishes such as varnish, although it must be pointed out here that shellac must only be used as a sealer under interior varnish and never exterior varnish no matter of what quality. Shellac is also used as a final finish in the form of french polish with gums added to surface quality furniture with either a full gloss or a matted-down finish. It is used as a spirit varnish in its own right and can be mixed with a proportion of plaster of paris, linseed oil and methylated spirits to produce a quick-drying filler.

The touching-up qualities are excellent – by using a little shellac plus methylated spirits and a pigment such as brown umber, the mixture can be used for high-lighting on surface coating, around knots etc. The surface of a french-polished finish is easily repaired, and faults such as rubs, burn marks, scratches, white rings etc. can be easily removed, whereas a similar fault on a modern surface is much more difficult to eradicate.

A french-polished finish can be applied either by mop, brush, rubber or spray-gun, yet durability and strength are long-lasting, due to its flexibility. Shellac does have some faults, and these the wood-finisher must understand. The finish is not water resistant, nor will it stand heat in any form (either dry or steam), and should not therefore be used for such items as bar tops, kitchen furniture and bathroom fittings or it will turn white and streaky. It must not be applied at temperatures under 60°F or blooming will take place, nor should it be applied as an exterior surface or sealer under, say, varnish or the finish will quickly deteriorate, and it also has a limited shelf life.

Shellac in recent years has undergone a fantastic price revision because of:

1. Hoarding of shellac by producers and distributors.
2. Climatic conditions not being favourable to the insects.
3. A demand by newer industries for shellac, other than the traditional paint and varnish users.
4. Problems of cultivation and the lack of incentive to "Lac" farmers. All these factors have made the world prices jump dramatically in recent years, and so the price of shellac-based materials are now compatable with cellulose products.

VARNISHING

Traditional resin oil varnishes have been used by man for many thousands of years. The early Greeks used varnish to preserve their wooden boats; the Egyptians used a great deal of varnish to coat and decorate their furniture and equipment as evidence of "finds" in their tombs have proven. Varnish was one of man's first "do-it-yourself" preserving and decorative finishes. The technique has been handed down to us and it is still applied in the same way – by brush.

What is varnish?

Varnish is a very loose term and nowadays does not mean any particular method or type of finishing. Many newer surface coatings, such as brush-on nitrocellulose lacquer, could be called a varnish simply because the method of application is by brushing on a transparent surface coating. One of the first text books written by John Stalker and George Parker and published in 1688 – "A Treatise of Japanning (Varnishing)" contained many formulas on how to make varnish.

In general terms then, it is a fairly thick fluid which, when applied by brush, covers a substrate with a resin floated within a medium which dries by evaporation. It thus protects and decorates wood with a hard surface coating which is waterproof. Traditionally a varnish is made up of (a) resins or gums – copal or arabic (the body), (b) mineral or vegetable oil – tung oil or linseed oil (the medium), (c) turpentine or white spirit (diluting fluid) and (d) driers – terebene (drying agent). Varnishes are, however, slow drying – even the polyurethane type taking 2-3 hours to dry, while the exterior type can take 6-12 hours to harden. This causes many problems for the finish, such as dust.

Types of varnish available

Synthetic varnish

In today's varnish manufacture, synthetic resins or alkyds, with longer-lasting qualities, are greatly used and most varnishes on the market contain alkyds in some form or another. They still do not last long enough – even a good quality external varnish properly applied and maintained only lasts for 3-5 years – though technology and research are greatly improving the life of these alkyd varnishes. They are frequently used for public buildings – banks and offices, as well as for the home and DIY market.

Traditional decorative varnish (interior use)

These had names in the past such as copal, church oak, cabinet – the descriptions are endless, but mainly today they are classified as decorative surface coatings. They are basically traditional in their make-up and are not intended for exterior use. Slow drying but mostly of a high gloss depth of resin, although some are satin or semi-matt. They have a high odour and are reasonably fast in drying – about 3-4 hours.

Decorative external varnish

These are supplied and named in various forms such as yacht varnish, sea-water resistant varnish, marine varnish, exterior varnish with ultra violet absorbent qualities and so on. These varnishes contain alkyd resins and are slow in drying but are very resistant against salt and sea spray and sea water so they are ideal for all situations that call for resistance to sea water or sea salt laden air.

Polyurethane varnish

These are very tough, flexible surface coatings and two main advantages over other varnishes are that: they dry by the absorption of ultra-violet light and thus they are touch-dry within the hour; and they are resistant against alkalis, acids, grease and alcohol so are ideal for bars and kitchen furniture.

The disadvantage of polyurethane varnish

Some polyurethane varnishes give off isocyanate fumes which are toxic during drying and application, so normal precautions must be observed such as good ventilation and face masks when working with them. In some cases eye shields are also advisable.

Flame retardant intumescent varnish

This is one of the new range of specialist varnishes produced to satisfy Building Regulations Specifications to give Class 1 ratings in accordance with BS 476 for use in public buildings such as schools, hotels, court rooms, churches etc. The finish can be either satin or gloss. Application is by brush or spray gun and the varnish is clear or translucent. One advantage of this type of varnish is that it has a low odour and contains no health hazards. The intention of an intumescent varnish is that if the surface comes under heat stress, it will not, like a normal traditional varnish burst into flames, but instead expand or swell for a period of at least half an hour.

Spirit varnish

These varnishes do not contain oil as the medium but "shellac", spirit or alcohol. Shellac varnishes are much thicker than ordinary shellac coatings and are applied by mop or brush. They dry very quickly and are bone dry in 1-2 hours.

Burnishing varnish

It is a little known fact that most varnishes will burnish to a mirror gloss. A final coat of varnish when dry – say after 14 days to be sure – will, in spite of all precautions show unsightly nibs, marks specks etc. These can be flatted with 600 grade silicon carbide wet and dry papers using soft water (rain or distilled) followed by burnishing using a proprietary burnishing polish. Best results are obtained by a power mop, but care has to be taken not to burn up the surface coating. First class results can be obtained in burnishing oil resin varnish.

Microporous varnish

This is one of the new breed of varnishes now on the market. This important development in varnish technology has made many well known paint and varnish manufacturers develop their own brand. The varnish is solely used on external woodwork and has no advantage if used internally. A microporous varnish is a mixture of organic and synthetic resins and oils blended to produce a fine varnish film which will outlast the more conventional external surface coatings. After application of three to four coatings, when dry the surface film allows the moisture from the wood to breathe through it. To put it another way the vapour from the wood passes through the varnish film thus during the winter when the wood moisture content is high, and in the summer when low the movement of the wood does not affect the varnish film. Some microporous varnishes contain colouring dyes and ultra-violet absorbers which help to protect the hard film from strong sunlight which is the enemy of all external surface coatings.

The advantages of microporous varnishes

1. Easy to apply in the normal pre-preparation and application brush procedures.
2. The varnish film allows moisture to pass through the dried film.

3. Gives maximum protection to external surfaces.
4. The film is flexible and elastic, which resists cracking.
5. Coloured varnishes contain light fast dyes which resist fading.

However, no surface coating applied externally will last forever – nor will these, but due to their special make up they will last for many years longer than ordinary varnishes. A great deal rests with the proper application and annual servicing of the surface to obtain the best out of any varnish.

Important oils

These are used by the wood finisher and used in the traditional make-up of varnishes:

Linseed oil

Raw linseed oil is obtained from the flax plant which is grown in such countries as India, Russia, USA, and Argentina. It is a light yellowish transparent coloured oil used: as a medium for varnishes, as a lubricant for french polishing by rubber, and as a wood protection in its own right (oiling technique) to oak, teak etc.

Boiled linseed oil

This is obtained by a "boiling" technique in manufacture. The oil becomes darkest brown and is mainly used in the manufacture of paint.

Both raw and boiled oils oxidize, but the boiled variety oxidizes more quickly than the raw.

Mineral oils

These can be termed "technical white oils". They are light transparent oils which are a by-product of the petrochemical industry, and can be used: as a lubricant for french polishing, as a plasticiser for use in fillers and lacquers, and as a protective wood finish on cedar shingle roof tiles etc.

Poppy oil

A vegetable oil obtained from the seed of poppies and used as a fine quality lubricant for french polishing rubbers or for oiling wood.

Tung oil or China wood oil

This oil from China is very quick drying and is used extensively in the manufacture of good quality exterior varnishes.

79

Castor oil

A vegetable oil extracted from the seeds of the castor plant or Palma Christi plant from the West Indies. This oil never dries out or oxidizes. It is used as a plasticiser and mainly added to cellulose lacquer to make brush-on lacquers. It also has medicinal uses!

White spirit or turpentine substitute

This is not a turpentine but a cheap solvent either added to cheap varnishes or paint or as a solvent to clean brushes. It is a product of the petrochemical industry and of mineral origin.

Teak oil

A man-made oil which is a mixture of vegetable and mineral oils and is applied by cloth to bare wood such as teak. All swabs of teak oil must be burned after use and must not be enclosed or the swabs could ignite. It is classed as a varnish.

Turpentine

"Venice" turpentine is one of the oldest-known turpentines, but it is only used as a traditional term. Turpentine is a vegetable oil solvent that dries by oxidation. There are two types: pure gum turpentine and gum turpentine. Pure gum turpentine, which is obtained by distillation from pitchy pine wood stumps is fairly economical to produce. Gum turpentine is a superior product produced by the exudation of gum resin from the long leaf pine tree. It is produced mainly in the southern USA, and is costly, but of the finest quality. It has a lovely scenty pine aroma.

Turpentines absorb oxygen thus forming a "film" – hence its use in the manufacture of paints and varnishes. It is also used in the manufacture of furniture wax polishes and creams, oil varnish and paint, oil stains, and in medicinal products – creams and ointments etc.

Applying external varnish to a pine softwood door

The correct way to use exterior varnish is described in this example. The preparation of the substrate must, of course, be carried out with meticulous care.
1. Sand down the pine door using 240 grade garnet papers and wipe down with methylated spirits to remove any grease etc.
2. If you intend to stain the wood then use a water stain as this type is light fast and will not fade. When dry, lightly sand down using 240 grade garnet papers as the water stain will slightly raise the grain.
3. Now apply one liberal coating of your chosen exterior varnish – this

coat must be thinned down by volume with 10% turpentine which is far better than white spirit because turpentine oxidizes, unlike white spirit. Allow this coating to dry hard. As it is of a thinner consistency the varnish will be absorbed into the fibres of the wood.

4. Sand down this surface using 240 grade garnet papers and dust off.
5. Now apply a second coating of your varnish, using it straight from the tin. Allow it to dry bone hard – about 2-3 days.
6. Using 600 grade silicon carbide papers (wet and dry) with soft water and a little soap, flat out the whole surface. Wipe down with clean water and dry off.
7. Apply a third and fourth coating of the varnish straight from the tin and allow to dry bone hard.
8. Depending on the quality of your workmanship, a further coating may be required. The final finish should look like glass and will last for many years. If required, the final finish can be burnished, but this must not be done less than two weeks after the final coating has dried.

A few tips on varnishing

1. Always use best quality exterior varnish or yacht varnish, or any reputable brand of exterior varnish.
2. Use best quality varnish brushes.
3. Use a good dusting brush and Tak rags to pick up dust before applying the varnish.
4. If any insects attach themselves to the wet film of varnish, leave them alone until the varnish is bone dry – then simply wash them off with warm water and burnish off.

FRENCH POLISHING

Some people say french polishing is an easy craft to master and all that is required is a little basic knowledge of the principles. This is not true. French polishing is an art if carried out to perfection. The time, patience, fortitude and devotion to putting a perfect finish onto the surface of a piece of bare wood takes just the same skill as a painter who applies paint to canvas. On the one hand the art is to beautify wood, and, on the other canvas.

What is french polishing? Once when I asked this question of a bunch of young students, back came the answer – "Doing a foreign job in Paris". Perhaps a less interesting but more accurate answer would be that it is applying a fluid made up of shellac – spirit and gums etc. all homogeneously mixed, which, when applied by a "rubber" to wood, results in a surface coating which is durable and artistic and has a gloss like glass.

Before proceeding further, let's look at the necessary materials required for french polishing.

Wadding

This is a soft fibre which is supplied in rolls and the beauty of this product is that it never congeals like ordinary cotton wool. It must however be emphasized that there are two types of wadding: the type used by upholsterers which has two outer skins and rough fibres and is no good for polishing usage, and the proper french polisher's wadding without skins which is softer for fads and rubbers.

Fads

A fad is simply a piece of wadding approximately 6″ square which is well worked in with methylated spirits and a little shellac and kept moist in a container ready for use. The fad itself is wadding made pear-shaped, and it is used simply to apply a coating of french polish onto a bare substrate, or for applying stains or sealers. It has no cloth covering at all, and new fads should never be used until they have been worn in a little in order to settle the minute fibres.

Rubbers

A rubber is the french polisher's most important "tool" and should be made with great care. A rubber is made from a piece of wadding – a fad in fact – which is boat or pear shaped, and is covered by a piece of absorbent cotton or linen cloth. It is again made with a pointed front end, and should not be round-shaped. All loose ends of the cloth should be tucked in or tied up so that they do not come into contact with the sole of the rubber. The rubber is a reservoir which holds a little of the french polish in proportion to the size of the job in hand. The operator holds the rubber and moves it along and around in circles and in figure eight movements, at the same time squeezing the body of the rubber gently to make the polish flow through the fibres of the covering cloth. Beginners and students take some time to master this technique as it is not as easy as it looks. A rubber is made up for the size of the job in hand – a small rubber for chair spindles for example, and a larger rubber for a dining room table. It should always be kept clean and moist and when not in use (even for five minutes), the rubber should always be kept in a glass or plastic jar with a large open neck and a good fitting lid. A good rubber is always a joy to use and will feel right – this cannot be described – and will last for weeks or even months if it is properly looked after. Wash out the cloth occasionally in methylated spirits and charge the wadding with french polish (never through the cloth), and always make up the rubber in a slightly different position as using the same area of the cloth will "clog up" the fibres and make the rubber useless. One main point I wish to emphasize is that the wadding of the rubber should always be taken out of the rubber to be re-charged with polish and gently pressed onto a clean piece of paper so that polish can be released before making it into a rubber. Beginners make the rubber drip with polish which is useless. The operator should be in full control of the rubber – it should not be too dry or too wet. Experience will dictate the correct amount of polish to use.

Applying french polish by rubber

Oils

There are two basic categories of oils – vegetable and mineral. These are used for lubricating the rubber and nothing else in the french polishing technique, and can be oils such as:

Raw Linseed Oil (not boiled) – the best grades of oil are those obtained from artists' material manufacturers as they are of purer quality.
Poppy Oil
Rape Oil
Mineral "White" Oil (which is actually transparent).

There are many others which can be used with the sole object of preventing the rubber from sticking to the surface while polishing.

Abrasive papers

A few examples are:
Garnet 240 grade (very fine)
Lubrisil 320 grade (very fine but lubricated with chalk)
Silicon Carbide 400-600 grade (wet and dry) which is used with linseed oil
0000 Steel Wool – ideal for flatting and dulling
Fine Pumice Powder – used for dulling or flatting with the beezer.

Other materials

Sulphuric Acid. – diluted in the proportion of 7 parts water to 1 part acid – used in the acid finish.

Vienna Chalk. This is a soft chalk of slaked lime containing magnesia – used in conjunction with sulphuric acid in the acid finish.

Rags. Muslin and paper towels. Used for all burnishing and general cleaning up.

Containers. These are most important. Glass or plastic jars with lids and an open neck (old honey jars) are ideal for the storage of rubbers, spiriting-off rubbers, acid finish rubbers, and fads
Note: they must all be stored separately.

Cotton Cloth or Linen Cloth. New cloth is useless. The cloth must be supple and have been well washed and have no dressing left in it or on it. Otherwise when made into a rubber, the polish will not flow through the fibres of the cloth and onto the wood.

Cotton cloth is produced from cotton, and linen cloth is produced from flax. Man-made-fibre cloth is not suitable.

Methylated Spirits. This is the actual spirit used to dissolve shellac flakes. It is a near-clear violet-tinted fluid made from alcohol wood spirits with added mineral spirits and colour which is methyl violet dye. Butyl alcohol is sometimes added to methylated spirits to meet special application conditions. Most manufacturers use industrial methylated spirits – known as IMS which is not obtainable by the general public.

French polish

This is made from a mixture of methylated spirits or IMS plus shellac flakes – other materials may be added such as gum benzoin, gum arabic, or copal – and a proportion of nitrocellulose to make better flow qualities. Ethyl cellulose can also be added to improve heat and moisture resistance. Basic french polishes are listed below.

Button polish

This is made from high grade orange shellac – the name "button" comes from the tradition of importing shellac in transluscent small size buttons of shellac. It is ideal for all coloured wood finishes such as mahogany, walnut etc.

Transparent French Polishes

(a) White French Polish. This is only white in appearance during bottle storage, but when applied to wood gives a transparent surface film. It is made from light coloured shellacs which are bleached and is ideal for such woods as pine, sycamore, beech etc.

(b) Pale or extra-pale french polishes. These are the true transparent polishes which are made from bleached light coloured shellacs. When these polishes are applied no discoloration at all is made to the woods and they are ideal for rosewood, teak, oaks etc.

Garnet french polish

This is a dewaxed dark coloured shellac which is ideal for all darker woods such as ebony, mahoganies etc. It sometimes has the prefix "AC Garnet" meaning Activated Carbonised in the dewaxing process by the manufacturer. It is not so popular nowadays as most furniture is finished lighter. This polish was made famous by many piano firms who used it on their instruments during the turn of the century. It also became popular with furniture makers of the period.

Coloured french polishes

These are french polishes of various basic shellacs with added spirit aniline dyes such as red, black, green, blue and so on. Any colour can be made to suit the situation.

Workshop procedure

This is a full workshop procedure for french polishing a substrate to full mirror gloss finish.

1. Prepare the surface of the substrate (Already described in detail in Chapter 9 – Filling grain).
2. Damp down with clean water to raise the grain.
3. When dry, sand down using 240 garnet abrasive papers.
4. Stain if required using a water stain.
5. Fill the grain if required using a wood grain filler.
6. Sand down slightly when fillers are dry.
7. Re-colour and allow to dry overnight.
   The substrate is now ready for french polishing.

Notes

The work area must not be damp, draughty, cold (the temperature should not be below 15°C), or dusty. The operator must wear protective clothing such as an apron or white nylon coat, and if possible a hat.

The object of these precautions is to eradicate as much as possible the hazards of dust and hairs dropping onto the surface of the work both from the operator's clothes and themselves.

Polishing

1. Take a fad and charge it with the french polish of your choice and go over the whole of the surface – with the grain, not across it. Allow to dry and repeat at least twice.
2. When dry after about two hours, flat down using 240 grade garnet papers but do not cut under the layer of polish. Dust off.
3. Take a rubber and charge the wadding with the correct amount of french polish and cover with a cloth, thus making a boat shaped rubber. Proceed now to "body in" – this is the equivalent of undercoating in painting – and what the polisher is doing is to give depth of polish to the surface. This takes time. Only work on the substrate for 10-15 minutes at any one time. Rub your rubber round and round and also use figure eight movements as well, making sure that every inch of the surface is polished or rubbed over. It is here in this process that a little lubricating oil is added to the sole of the rubber, otherwise it will stick and seize up. It must be emphasised that when finishing a polishing session, you must rub off in the direction of the grain to eradicate the swirls or "spiders" of polishing rubber marks. The object of using a lubricating oil with the rubber is simply to ease the movement of the rubber cloth over the surface of the wood. Do not overdo the use of oil, but do not starve it either – it is a happy balance which comes with practice. Vegetable oils in my opinion are better than mineral oils, but it is a matter of personal choice.
4. Allow each coating of polish during the bodying in technique to fully dry out. A good yardstick is for every fifteen minutes of polishing, allow 2 hours to harden off. It is only when a good surface of hard polish has dried out that the beezer is used.

The beezer (see chapter 16 – Flatting)

Spread raw linseed oil over the substrate and, using a pounce bag, lightly apply a dusting of fine pumice powder. Grind the oil and pumice together using slight pressure on the beezer to do this. The object is to flat or grind the whole surface of the polished area. Use a circular motion and make sure you do not cut into any edges of the substrate or cut too deep into the skin of the french polish. Wipe the whole area with a clean rag and inspect the surface. It will be a matt finish and will be perfectly flat – if it isn't – repeat the whole process with the beezer until it is! There should be no shiny areas showing.

After wiping off all traces of oil and pumice, proceed to "body in" but use a 50% thinned mixture of french polish and methylated spirits. Finish off in straight strokes with the grain and leave to dry out for at least 24 hours.

Spiriting off

After the surface has dried for at least 6-24 hours, proceed to spirit off, which simply means to use methylated spirits (or better still "finishing off spirit" which contains resins) to remove all traces of the oil which is smearing the surface. Simply charge a piece of wadding with a little finishing spirit and make into a rubber, then, using straight strokes in the direction of the grain carry on working until your rubber is almost dry and then leave to dry out.

Some polishers use the original rubber for spiriting off and some use a separate one – the choice is up to the operator but I prefer the latter simply because it is cleaner and there is no polish or oil present on the cloth.

Patience and fortitude are required during spiriting off and skill in the operation of this process which only comes with practice. The result is a gloss surface free of oil streaks, if the process is carried out correctly. It is a good idea to allow the finished spirited surface to harden up for a day or so before touching or using the surface. If by any chance after a few days some slight oil smears re-appear (due to the oil oxidizing), then apply the spiriting off rubber again, but only use a very little spirit in this instance.

There is yet another way of eradicating surplus oil on the surface of a french polished surface and that is the *Acid finish*. This is mainly used in conjunction with the "piano finish" which is aimed at producing a perfect flat full mirror gloss french polished finish. There is one basic requirement if using either the spiriting off or acid technique and that is that the bodying in surface thickness is as near perfect as possible and that after any polishing the surface must be left for at least 6-10 hours to dry out hard.

The acid finish

Liberally charge the wadding of a new rubber with dilute sulphuric acid (7 parts of water to 1 part of acid). The dilution must be carried out well

before usage, as heat is produced on dilution. It should be allowed to cool down before use, and should then be wiped onto the surface of the polish. Immediately dust on Vienna chalk using a pounce bag – there is no need for the pounce bag to touch the substrate – simply use it like a pepper pot to dust the surface.

Using the rubber in straight strokes in the direction of the grain wipe over the surface of the substrate. The polish at this stage will turn matt and slightly muddy, but carry on until the rubber in conjunction with the Vienna chalk clears the surface of all traces of lubricating oil which has been applied during the "bodying in" sessions. The Vienna chalk itself acts as a mild burnishing agent and polishes the polish.

It takes practice to achieve this fantastic mirror gloss "piano finish" which will look and feel like glass – no other technique will do this as the surface of the french polish has had all traces of oil removed by a chemical reaction produced by the oil, acid and Vienna chalk combined.

Leave the substrate to harden for at least 7-14 days at a room temperature not below 65°F before normal usage.

There is one effect in french polishing that is desirable in some circumstances – that is a dull or matt finish. At the "bodying in" stage of the process simply spirit off using a finishing spirit and allow to dry out hard. The choice now is the method of dulling the gloss surface film.

(a) Fine Pumice Powder. This is dusted onto the surface. Using a piece of muslin, rub in the direction of the grain and the gloss finish will quickly disappear leaving a dull finish. Dust off all surplus pumice powder – some operators use a soft brush like a shoe brush to achieve the effect.

(b) 000 or 0000 Steel Wool. Cut a piece of 000 or 0000 fine steel wool and gently rub all over the gloss surface. This results in a fine smooth matt or dull finish.

Antique finish

An antique surface finish is achieved by first french polishing up to "bodying in", leaving to dry hard for at least six hours and then simply using fine steel wool of 0000 grade in conjunction with a standard wax furniture polish. Rub well into the french polished surface and finally wipe off all surplus wax polish with a clean muslin cloth.

MODERN WOOD FINISHING AND SPRAY GUNS

Cellulose-based surface coatings

Although there is still a great deal of traditional wood finishing being practised, most furniture produced today is finished with modern industrial surface coatings and these are classified as "Modern Wood Finishing".

The main surface coatings in common use throughout the world are:
1. Nitrocellulose lacquers (known as N/C lacquers)
2. Pre-catalysed lacquers (known as pre-cat lacquers)
3. Acid hardened lacquers (known as A/C lacquers)
4. Polyurethane lacquers (known as P.U. lacquers)
5. Polyester lacquers (known as unsaturated polyester lacquers)

Each one of these finishes will be dealt with in detail, but first of all note that these finishes are chemically produced and unlike traditional finishes have very low flash points. This makes them highly flammable, and in some instances dangerous to use, so they must be used with great care.

During the middle part of this century, cellulose was obtained mainly from the chemical reaction of acids on cotton linters or waste cotton floss. As demand grew, wood pulp from certain trees was used instead of cotton, and the Monterey pine, spruce, western hemlock and the newest South African eucalyptus (a fast-growing tropical tree) have now become an important source of cellulose.

The wood surface coating manufacturers are but one of the many consumers of this vast industry which produces cellulose raw material using modern technology. The USA and South Africa are the two main countries who specialize in this source of production.

Nitrocellulose lacquer (a reversible finish)

This really should be called Cellulose Nitrate. This popular surface coating for any wood substrate is basically made up of:
1. Nitrocellulose (the derivative or chemical substance).
2. Resins (to build lustre, toughness and adhesion).
3. Plasticisers (to increase flexibility and mixing properties).
4. Softeners or thinners (to make the liquid flow and evaporate the solvent).

This basic materials produce a surface coating which is clear and flexible when dry. The flash point of this material is normally low.

Advantages of a nitrocellulose lacquer

1. The surface film at any time during its lifetime can be pulled over.
2. It is fast drying – touch dry within 30 minutes at 65°F and fully hard within 48 hours at the same temperature.
3. It has a full range of compatible sealers, thinners and toners.
4. It is an ideal material for burnishing (after pullovering), using a powered polishing mop with various abrasive cellulose burnishing preparations.
5. It is highly soluble – mixes well with thinners, french polish, toners, methylated spirits.
6. It is ideal for spray or machine coating – also can be brushed on or used with dip methods.
7. It is reasonably resistant against alcohol, water, heat.
8. It can be obtained in gloss, semi-gloss (satin) or matt finishes.
9. Damaged surfaces can be repaired easier than any other cellulose based surface coating.
10. It is best suited for domestic usage.
11. It can be sprayed on vertical substrates with ease.

Disadvantages of a nitrocellulose lacquer

1. It dries too quickly, rendering it difficult to flow easily over large areas.
2. Due to low flashpoint, the surface film has fire hazards and hence it cannot be used on aircraft, railway carriages or other public conveyances.
3. Surface film when drying has a tendency to sink due to the 25-30% low solid cellulose content of the material, thus requiring further coatings.
4. A "haze" can form on the surface due to many temperamental instances.
5. Popular oil stains tend to bleed through this surface coating and should not be used.
6. While slightly resistant to many hazards, the dried film is not really recommended for "hard usage" items such as table tops where commercial usage is envisaged.

Pre-catalysed lacquer (or cold cure lacquer)

This is a most popular form of modern surface coating for wood substrates. It is a combination of urea-formaldehyde, nitrocellulose, melamine and alkyd resins (synthetic) and it contains the catalyst ready mixed or pre-mixed at the manufacturing stage. The flash point of this material is normally below 73°F. It is an ideal surface coating for all kitchen furniture, table tops, dressing tables, coffee tables etc. where great usage is envisaged. It is far superior to nitrocellulose and is known universally as a "one-pack" or pre-cat lacquer.

Advantages of a pre-catalysed lacquer

1. It has a much higher resistance than nitrocellulose to abrasions, alcohol, and wet and dry heat.
2. It has a good drying speed – touch dry within 30-45 minutes.
3. After drying out for 30-45 minutes it can be flatted and re-coated if required.
4. It can be "pulled over" within 1-2 hours of initial drying (not later).
5. It is ideal for any wood substrate.
6. It is ideal for spraying and machine coating application.
7. It can be obtained in tinted, clear, pigmented and in gloss satin or matt.

Disadvantages of a pre-catalysed lacquer

1. Nitrocellulose sanding sealers and thinners cannot be used.
2. Oil stains should not be used under this surface coating unless thinly coated with de-waxed shellac sealer.
3. It takes up to 5-7 days to fully cure before using the surface.
4. It has a limited container shelf life (approximately 8 months).
5. There must be a limited surface thickness of coatings – 2-3 coatings maximum.
6. The surface film when cured in non-reversible.
7. The surface is difficult and often impossible to touch-up and repair damages.
8. After drying for two hours or more, the surface cannot be "pulled over" (unlike nitrocellulose).
9. Sealers containing zinc stearates (used in most sanding sealers) must *never* be used as the catalyst will react with the metallic stearate, thus cracking up the surface.

Acid-catalysed (two-pack) lacquer

This lacquer is supplied in concentrated form but when put to use requires an acid to be mixed (normally 1 part of acid to 10 parts of lacquer with a little thinner, but this can vary). Once mixed, the surface coating sprayed onto a substrate will dry by chemical reaction of the acid acting as the catalyst, thus producing a very hard-wearing film of exceptional build and flow properties. It is a non-reversible surface coating once dry and cured.

Advantages of acid-catalysed lacquer

1. It can be used on varied substrates and is ideal for commercial furniture – school furniture etc.

2. It can be obtained in clear or pigmented finishes in gloss, satin or matt finishes.
3. At 65°F approximately A/C lacquers will skin off in ½ hour and will be touch dry within 60 minutes.
4. It can be re-coated within two hours.
5. It has a high solid content of lacquer of 45%.
6. It withstands heat, alcohol, abrasions, alkalis better than other finishes.
7. It has a higher flash point than other finishes – below 90°F.
8. The film does not sink when dry.
9. It can be easily burnished when fully cured.
10. It has a faster curing time when pre-cat lacquer (approximately 4 days).
11. Some manufactured A/C lacquers do not require base-sanding sealers.

Disadvantages of acid-catalysed lacquer

1. It will not stand up to wet heat or external exposure, nor will it withstand strong alkalis.
2. The cured film is non-reversible, thus making it extremely difficult to repair damages.
3. It cannot be "pulled over" at any time during the application process, or, in fact, anytime.
4. Special compatible thinners are required (pre-cat or nitrocellulose thinners are not suitable).
5. No sanding sealers can be used.
6. Shellac sealers must not be used.

Polyurethane lacquer

Polyurethane lacquers are two-pack lacquers. They have excellent adhesion, good flexibility, and are heat, water, acid, alkali and alcohol resistant. They can be formulated to suit various situations and are suitable for a great many wooden substrates. They are supplied in clear gloss, matt or satin – tinted or pigmented finishes.

Advantages of polyurethane lacquers

1. They are free from surface sinkage.
2. They have a high resistance to heat, water, alcohol, acid and alkaline substances.
3. They are fast drying – dust free in 10-15 minutes and touch dry in 2 hours.
4. They have a very high flash point – below 90°F and are hence much safer to use than other lacquers.
5. They can be used as additives, for example to nitro-cellulose binders for woodfillers – (ideal under A/C lacquer).
6. They can be sprayed, machine surface coated or fadded.

Disadvantages of polyurethane lacquers

1. When catalyst is added and during curing, isocyanate fumes can be given off. This is a major hazard, and therefore special masks must be worn.
2. It is extremely important that the correct ratio of catalyst be measured.
3. Special thinners and sealers must be used which do not contain alcohol or water absorbing solvents.
4. The final curing can take up to seven days – a drawback on a production line volume work.
5. When fully-cured the surface is non-reversible and impossible to repair surface faults.

Polyester finish

This is the king of plastic coated surfaces. It is a specialist surface which looks like thick glass or plastic forming a covering encasement of the wood. It is a unique non-reversible finish because unlike all the other lacquers mentioned, all the liquid that is applied to a wood substrate becomes solid and there is very little or no solvent loss. It can be applied to any wood substrate including laminates and is used extensively by furniture manufacturers and by the piano industry and also for radio and T.V. cabinets, car facia panels, kitchen units, electronic organs etc. It is a very sophisticated finish demanding experience and skill in the production of the finish.

Advantages of a polyester finish
(Wax-type two-pack system catalyst-hardened).
1. Needs next to no servicing – just a dry cloth to remove dust and finger grease.
2. It has a high flash point – below 90°F.
3. The solvent becomes part of the film-forming surface coating.
4. It requires very low spray-gun pressure – 20-25 p.s.i.
5. No sealers or primers are required.
6. It can be burnished with powered edge mops with ease.
7. It is resistant to wet, heat, acid, alkali, alcohol.
8. There is no solvent loss and therefore no sinkage.
9. Dries hard within a minimum of 6 hours – the latest ultra-violet cured polyester can dry in 10 seconds using special equipment.
10. It is a very durable film in both clear matt and gloss.
11. Various coatings can be applied within minutes of each other.

Disadvantages of a polyester finish

1. Spray guns must be cleaned within approximately 20 minutes of mixing a catalyst or activator.
2. A non-reversible finish.

3. To produce a gloss finish the surface must be burnished with abrasive pastes, unlike other lacquers, that produce a finished gloss film from the gun.
4. The surface chips like glass and is virtually impossible to repair on large surfaces like piano lids etc.
5. It has a very short spray gun or pot life – 15-20 minutes on mixing catalyst, and leaving it in the gun for too long renders it useless.
6. It cannot be applied to vertical surfaces.
7. It must be flatted down prior to burnishing.
8. It requires great skill and very expensive plant to produce this finish and is therefore purely a commercial type of wood surface finish.
9. Face masks must be worn when "spraying" this lacquer.

Spray gun technique for wood finishes

Great mistrust is unfortunately still attached to the spray gun by many, but for applying wood finishing liquids such as paint, or modern finishes such as nitrocellulose, pre-catalysed, acid-catalysed polyurethane and polyester lacquers onto wood substrates, it cannot be bettered. Dipping tanks and surface coating machines have their place in industrial finishing and some operators still use brushing lacquers, but the spray gun method of application requires very little space to operate, is an excellent method of applying surface coatings and a completely first class result can be achieved.

First of all the appropriate safety measures need to be brought into practice and these have been previously described. Most or all of them are common sense, the main ones being concerned with fire prevention, ventilation and the extraction of over-spray fumes.

The spray gun, when operating, consists of two important components: the gun head with container which holds the liquid surface coating and the compressor, normally run by electricity, which produces the actual "air" pressure the gun requires. The air pressure so produced is fed by a hose, normally of rubber, from the compressor to the gun head so that an adequate volume of air is available which incidentally must be dry and clean and preferably filtered against oil and water infiltration which produces many surface faults.

The basic principle of spraying surface coatings is to break up a volume of liquid – be it paint, lacquer etc. into small atomised particles by using air pressure, and to reproduce the particles through the fine jet on the gun head into a liquid which can then be deposited onto a suitably prepared substrate in a flat wet film, evenly distributed over the surface. When dry, this film of surface coating should be as free as possible from any foreign particles such as hairs, dust (nibs), cissing or surplus fluid runs and other surface faults. This will take skill and practice to achieve, but care and patience plus good clean equipment which is properly maintained will bring about the desired result.

Viscosity

All finishing surface coatings are normally packed either in 5 or 25 litre

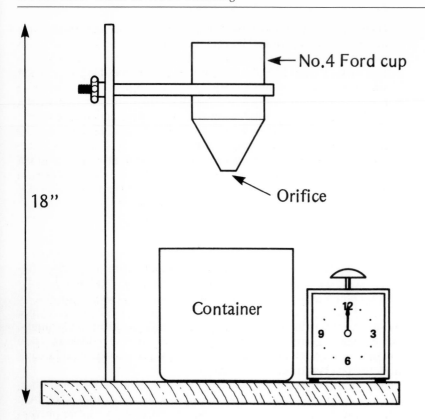

← No.4 Ford cup

Orifice

18"

Container

containers and are in concentrated solutions. They must however be thinned down to be able to be sprayed onto a substrate or used in surface coating machines, and in order to satisfy certain manufacturer's specifications for various substrates these surface coatings must be thinned down accurately.

Viscosity is termed as "resistance to flow" and is used to define the accurate consistency to which the basic surface coating fluid is mixed or thinned down. This is to allow it to flow through the spray gun or the surface coating machine, and re-form in a perfect, controlled wet film prior to hardening according to the manufacturer's instructions. This rules out guesswork, and the correct viscosity is obtained.

There are various ways of obtaining an accurate viscosity of a surface coating fluid. One very popular way is to use a flowcup known as the No. 4 Ford Cup. Room temperature is important when testing for viscosity and must be kept constant throughout the surface coating operation. Normally the work area temperature should be in the region of 75°F.

Acquiring the correct viscosity

Whatever you are using, the manufacturer of the lacquer, synthetic coating, polyurethane or polyester etc., will give the viscosity required. A known viscosity factor is therefore given of the correct amount of thinning required. Using a No. 4 Ford Cup device (see diagram), place a finger over the orifice at the bottom of the cup and then fill the cup with the surface coating fluid. Draw a spatula across the top of the cup to level off the liquid (this is important). Place a container under the cup and at the same time release the finger and start a second's stop clock. As soon as the stream of fluid in the cup breaks up, stop the clock. The fluid is further thinned and the process is repeated until the cup is emptied at the time stated by the specifications of the surface coating. Further adjustments are made until the cup is emptied exactly on the specified time. This is then the viscosity of the fluid which will flow, dry, harden and cure correctly as the manufacturer intended, which is not possible if guesswork is used.

Hot spray lacquer

This is a method of spraying a lacquer which is heated prior to spraying onto a substrate. The lacquer is of a special type not suitable for cold curing spraying techniques, but upon heating in a special type of spray gun or pressure pot either by electric element or by circulatory hot water; the lacquer can then be sprayed. It must be emphasized that the equipment is of a special design for the application of hot lacquer only and ordinary cold spraying equipment must never be used or adapted for hot spraying usage.

A cold cure lacquer can be sprayed at a viscosity of say 60 seconds using a No. 4 B.S. cup as testing measurement of the mixture of lacquer and solvents, but to increase the solid content to say 90 seconds would make the lacquer unsprayable. If however the high content low viscosity lacquer at 90 seconds was heated to 120/149F (52.9/65C) thus reducing the viscosity to say 45 seconds this would make the lacquer sprayable.

The Advantages of a Hot Lacquer System

1. Can be used with cellulose lacquer or synthetic enamels, primers, undercoats etc.
2. Better coverage and a far better and heavier surface coating
3. Much easier to apply to vertical surfaces due to less solvent being present within the lacquer
4. A good 50% saving on solvents and labour time
5. Thermostatically controlled pots prevent over-heating of the lacquer (cuts out at 65C) thus the consistency is constant
6. A lower PSI can be used
7. Less surface faults such as orange peel, fatty edges, sags and runs, cissing etc.
8. Less dust contamination of the surface
9. Quicker drying due to less solvent being present within the lacquer
10. The spray results to substrates are consistent throughout the temperature changes of the day within the work area particularly during cold or winter periods

Disadvantages of a hot lacquer

1. Extra costs involved due to special designed equipment
2. Extra costs due to electricity for heating the pots
3. Special low viscosity and high flash point lacquer must be used
3. Certain extra fire precautions need to be observed
4. Skilled spray operators are necessary
5. Can only be used for small operation work
6. Overspray is more costly than ordinary cold cure lacquers

Modern lacquers are best applied by spray gun, or surface coating machine, for large concerns and there are many excellent models on the market today ranging in price from £150 to £1,000, which are ideal for the small operator wishing to obtain professional results.

Three main types are available:
1. Gravity Feed Guns – ideal for flat surface horizontal substrates such as table tops etc.
2. Suction Pressure Feed Guns – ideal for vertical surface substrates such as panels, doors etc.
3. Electric Airless Guns – ideal for the DIY enthusiast.

Gravity feed guns

A gravity feed gun has the surface coating fluid above the jets. It depends on an internal air cushion to create an unbroken stream of atomized fluid, and its air supply comes from an electrically driven compressor producing 100 lbs per square inch (p.s.i.) adjustable to 50 p.s.i. for general spraying purposes. The gun is ideal for spraying slow-drying fluids, paint, fillers, sealers, undercoats, and cellulose lacquers – both pigmented and clear. In large production shops, a bulk supply of surface coating material being sprayed is kept in a centralized tank which can feed various spray guns. The tank is fitted with its own pressure gauge which ensures consistency of supply to each gun, yet can be adjusted by each individual operator.

Suction pressure feed spray guns

A pressure feed type gun is powered by an electric compressor unit working at approximately 60 p.s.i. which directs pressure from the air hose into a sealed fluid container, forcing fluid up the fluid tube. The "bleeder" type in this group releases air through the nozzle continuously. Pressing the trigger releases the fluid into the nozzle where it is atomized and sprayed by the air stream. This type of gun is ideal for spraying shellac, varnish, lacquer, paints, and enamels onto vertical surfaces.

Airless electric spray guns

These are more suitable to the DIY enthusiast or amateur. This type of

A gravity feed spray gun – ideal for mass production work on flat, horizontal surfaces

gun operates by finely atomizing all sprayable materials by hydro-static, high pressure. After passing through a nozzle system these atomized particles are delivered onto the surface by a very efficient electric pump within the jet area.

The great advantages of an airless gun are:

1. There is less overspray (although this does vary from manufacturer to manufacturer).
2. There is a saving on fluid finishes of about 70% due to the above.
3. Spraying can be carried out easily "on site", provided that there is an electricity supply.
4. The units are very small, compact and portable. The "Wagner" High Pressure Spray Gun plus attachments are supplied in a steel box which measures 15″ x 10 ″.

A suction feed gun – ideal for vertical surfaces, and often used in the motor trade

The only disadvantage of this type of gun is the extra weight, bulk and noise of the actual spray gun operation.

Technique of using spray guns

1. The distance of gun to surface should be about 7″ to 9″.
2. Use straight smooth strokes (no arc line).
3. Keep the triggering and movement steady.
4. Use deep lapping or spray past the object.
5. Keep the equipment surgically clean at all times.
6. Before spraying onto a substrate, try it first on a spare piece of ply-wood, making all the necessary adjustments.

A portable auto-controlled spray compressor unit – ideal for the small operator, it simply plugs in a 13amp socket

Safety precautions

When operating any type of spray gun, there are a few safety precautions to follow.
1. Use a face mask at all times when spraying surface coatings.
2. Provide adequate ventilation – either open doors or windows or an extractor fan. The air should be replaced every two minutes.
3. Make sure that *no* naked flame is burning while spraying. This means no oil heaters, gas fires, open fires etc. Remember that the fumes from lacquers have very low flashpoints which are equal to those from petrol.

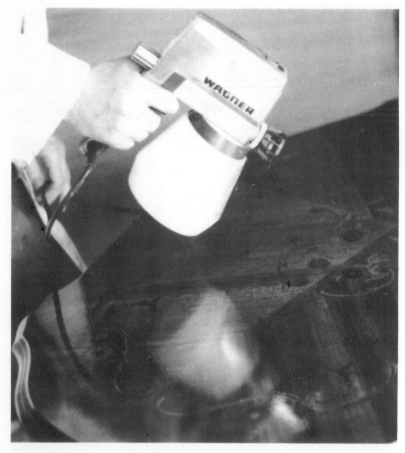

4. Make sure that neither the operator nor anyone else in the work area is smoking.
5. Do not keep or consume food or drink in the spraying area.

Spray finishing

Having chosen a suitable type of spray gun, you will now be wondering what finish to apply. If you look at modern furniture, you will discover that there are three basic finishes:
1. Satin finishes with open grain or filled grain.
2. Gloss with open grain (not filled) or full mirror gloss (filled grain).
3. Matt finishes with filled or open grain.
   As a rough guideline, reproduction furniture in mahogany or sapele woods are gloss finished whereas teak and oak on modern furniture are satin or matt finished – it is a matter of fashion with manufacturers.

Common Surface Film Faults

To achieve a fine, smooth, evenly-applied surface coating the spray

Two popular face masks used when spraying cellulose surface coatings

gun operator must learn to avoid many pitfalls. There are many faults and defects that can occur, and here are just a few of the more common and important ones with hints on how to eradicate or avoid them.

Cratering or Cissing

This is the sprayer's nightmare, and looks like a close-up picture of the moon. It can be caused by:
1. Oil or water moisture in the air lines from the compressor to the spray gun head.
2. Minute particles of wax or silicones in the air, while spraying.
3. Minute amounts of paint stripper fumes (such as methylene chloride or ammonia).
4. Oil stains or other non-compatible materials being used, such as when ammonia is mixed with water stains to help penetration.

To rectify

1. Clean out air lines or fit a moisture filter to the hose near the gun head.
2. Make sure no other fumes, such as silicone sprays, are nearby.
3. Use the correct stains, such as water stains containing no ammonia.
4. If cissing does occur while the film is still wet, use a tooth pick to drop the same lacquer from the gun into the cavities, and then flat down when dry. If too many cissed craters occur, simply strip off and respray.

Rucking

This looks like the effect of paint stripper on a surface film. It occurs

Open grain gloss finish

Filled grain full gloss finish

Filled grain matt finish

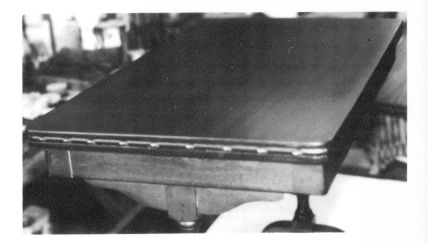

when applying a second coating of lacquer to a near-polymerised hardened surface film. The solvents in the lacquer attack the semi-hardened film and this swells up and lifts from the substrate.

To rectify

1. If too bad the whole surface must be stripped and re-applied.
2. Extend the recommended drying time to help complete polymerisation of the first coating before applying the second.
3. Make sure that the correct catalyst ratio has been mixed if using A/C lacquers.

Chilling

Chilling is caused by moisture in the air condensing onto the dry surface coating.

To rectify

1. Improve the workshop or spray area temperature to approximately 75°F.
2. Avoid sudden draughts.
3. Clean out the air line moisture filter or, in the case of small units, clean out the pressure air tanks.

Nibs

The enemy of any wood finish, these are small particles of dust, hairs or particles of fibre from pre-sanding (including dandruff from the operator) being trapped either within or on top of the surface coating.

To rectify

1. The substrate must be clean and dust absorbing "tak" rags used.
2. Suitable clean protective clothing should be worn.
3. The working area should be absolutely clean, including bench tops and floors.
4. To remove the nibs, use suitable abrasive papers. The silicon carbide type wet or dry 400/600 grades can be used with soft water (rain) and a little soap; or white spirit. Otherwise use the dry "Lubrisil" fine 320 grade paper.

Orange Peel

This is a common fault when using the spray gun in a vertical position and is caused by too heavy a coating of surface lacquer in a certain area. The heavy spraycoat builds up into an overladen peel – hence the description.

To rectify

1. The film must be bone dry before normal flatting takes place using wet and dry methods.
2. Pullovering will help, or a respray over.

Printing or flooding

This is when a small area on a large substrate is still showing signs of being wet after the initial drying time has elapsed. The surface coating has been applied too heavily in certain spots. The solvents are thus trapped by the wet surface.

To rectify

1. Leave extra time for drying.
2. Increase workshop temperature to 65-75°F.
3. Apply gentle heat (hot air type) to the trouble spots.
4. If an A/C lacquer has been used, wipe over with a fad of the catalyst. Check for the correct ratio of this catalyst if further spraying has to be done.

Blooming or haze

Nitrocellulose films are prone to this defect, particularly the full gloss finishes. This haze effect can occur after a few days when the surface film has completely hardened.

To rectify

1. Use an anti-haze remover (a cream reviver containing french chalk)

if the surface is a fully-filled one. Do not use on an open-grain film.
2. Use a non-blooming type of lacquer and thinner.
3. Check workshop temperature is not below 65°F.

Spray booths

When using any spray gun, the removal of overspray air contamination fumes is essential. These can be disposed of, or minimised, by using extractor fans, air blow fans, adequate ventilation; or a spray booth.

The type of system used depends on the product. For example, a small concern spray-finishing coffee tables would require a small spray booth, while a concern spray-finishing 12′ refectory tables would require a very large extractor system. Spray booths are generally custom built to suit the furniture concerned, and there are two types: "Dry back" or "water wash" spray booths.

The dry back booth

This is a metal cubicle with an extractor fan and exhaust tube outlet at the back. The sides of the metal cubicle are sprayed with a flexible type film which is really a non-adhesive, latex-based, fire-resistant skin. When the skin absorbs too much overspray, it is simply peeled off and renewed. This skin film is also used by film companies for set coverings etc. In each booth there is an overhead sealed light unit and a metal turn-table so that substrates can be revolved and the actual spraying directed to the back of the booth at all times.

The water wash booth

There are various types, but they basically consist of a metal cubicle like the dry back type, but with a continuous stream of water flowing from the top to the bottom at the back of the booth. The water is continuously pumped back up to the top to circulate, and is also mixed with a softening agent to prevent clogging through the pipes. There is also an extractor, a fan-light (sealed), and again the metal sides of the booth are latex-coated. A metal turn-table is generally available so that the spraying action is directed to the back of the booth into the stream of water.

The main advantage of spray booths are:
1. Face masks are not required by operators (so those who wear spectacles are greatly assisted).
2. Health and fire hazards are greatly reduced.
3. No overspray fumes pollute the rest of the work area.
4. They are essential for polyester and polyurethane lacquer application.
5. All spray fumes are immediately dispersed or absorbed into the stream of water (according to the type of booth being used).

BURNISHING AND PULLOVERING

Pullovering is a technique in modern wood finishing using cellulose-based products, and should not be confused with "finishing-off" in french polishing. The process has nothing at all to do with traditional shellac-based wood finishing.

It is a method of applying a slow or fast acting diluting fluid to the surface film by a hand rubber. The same type is used as that by french polishers, made of wadding covered by a piece of absorbent white cotton cloth. The pullover process is carried out on a gloss surface only, either nitrocellulose lacquer or pre-catalysed lacquer. The pull-over solution fluid consists of a mixture of solvents which dilute the surface film for just long enough to slide over – hence the term "pull-over" – the surface skin with the object of producing a fine "re-flowed" mirror gloss finish. The process must be carried out after flatting to remove all surface faults such as nibs, cissing, or heavy runs, and requires skill and practice to carry out. There are two qualities of pull-over fluids. The milder types have a slower dissolving action and are for use on surfaces such as nitrocellulose lacquers. The stronger solutions are used on the pre-catalysed lacquers, because they have a faster dissolving action. Not all cellulose-based lacquers can be pulled over: acid catalyst lacquers, polyester and polyurethane lacquers are all unsuitable for the process. Pullover would have no effect at all on them due to the "hardness" of the surface coating. Nitrocellulose is the ideal lacquer for pulling over because of its reversibility, and this can be carried out at any stage, either just after the initial drying or weeks or even months later. This is not so, however, with pre-catalysed lacquers when the process must be carried out no later than 2-3 hours after the initial touch-drying of the surface film, or great difficulty will result in trying to pullover. The longer a pre-catalysed lacquer is left – up to a maximum of seven days due to the non-reversibility – the harder it becomes. A pullover solution is made chemically and for a nitrocellulose lacquer film the following mild pullover solution is thus formulated:–

Special Petroleum Ethers	– 50%	(by volume)
Methylated Spirits	– 25%	"
Butyl Acetate	– 10%	"
Butyl Alcohol	–10%	"
Toluol	– 5%	"

The spray gun is normally used to apply cellulose lacquers on furni-

Pullovering – a walnut veneer table top

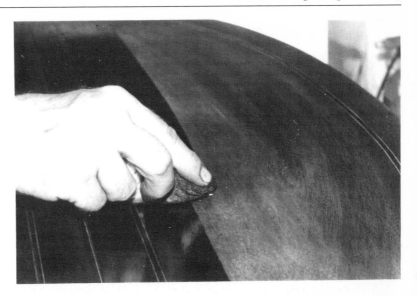

ture these days, but for those not used to the technique of spraying, there are lacquers specially made to brush on. These are somewhat thicker and are slower to dry, but the resultant coating is somewhat thicker in depth. A greater depth of de-nibbing and removal of brush faults can therefore be carried out. Pullovering is essential with this method of applying lacquer, in order to obtain a really good finish.

Repairing damaged to cellulose surfaces

Pullovering is used by skilled operators in repairs to cellulose surfaces (not pre-catalysed or acid-catalysed as these are non-reversible surfaces). Nitrocellulose is very easily repaired after treating for damage, such as marks or chips, and slightly flatting down the repaired area. The surface can be pullovered to restore it to its original glory. Normally the process is used on full gloss finishes, but can be undertaken on satin surfaces as long as a satin respray is carried out after pullovering or fine steel wool is used to dull down the high gloss produced by pulling over.

How to use the pullover technique

1. Charge the rubber wadding with pullover fluid. It should not be dripping wet, just enough to well-moisten the wadding. Cover the wadding with absorbent cloth and make into a rubber in the normal way.
2. Make sure that the substrate has been de-nibbed and all other surface faults and all dust removed.
3. Start at the bottom and work upwards by using straight strokes in the direction of the grain, either from right to left or left to right to suit the operator. Keep the rubber moving at all times, do not stop or

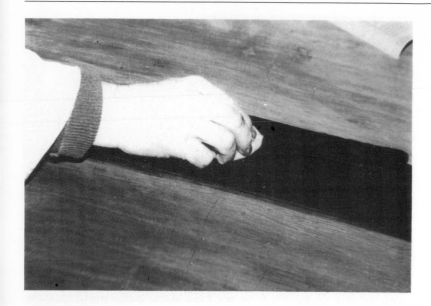

Close-up shows rubber in use with a pullover solution on a Nitrocellulose lacquer full gloss finish

start midway on the surface. Proceed with this action until the surface becomes glossy and looks perfect. It will take time and skill to master the technique.

4. Use the rubber until it dries up, then leave the surface to dry out for about 4-6 hours.

Helpful tips on pullovering

1. Do not have your rubber too saturated with pullover solution.
2. Try not to pullover on the same spot or area for too long or the surface will tear up.
3. Do not start your rubber midway on the substrate, but start one end and finish the other.
4. Do not use your rubber across the grain but *always* with the direction of the grain.
5. When pullovering allow 6-12 hours for drying before packing or using.
6. Keep your rubbers in a glass or plastic container when not in use and keep separate from french polish rubbers.
7. Remember that pullover solution has a very low flashpoint – so no smoking and no naked flames while the process is being carried out.
8. Have good ventilation as the fumes are quite strong and toxic.

Burnishing to a gloss finish

There are two aims in burnishing cellulose-based surfaces: to eliminate coarse scratches or minor faults until they are not visible; and to re-flow the top surface skin by heat generated by the friction of either a hand-held cloth or power mop.

Burnishing – a powered mop used on a grand piano lid with a Nitrocellulose gloss finish

Hand burnishing a gloss finish rosewood table top

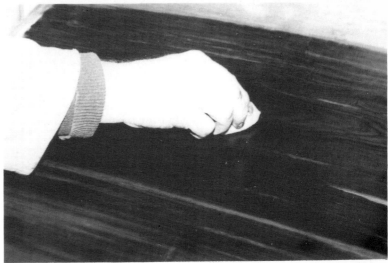

Burnishing is carried out with a burnishing paste and a piece of washed mutton cloth, or a power mop for large surfaces such as grand piano lids or table tops. A power mop consists of a rotary head with a lambswool or felt bonnet.

After a surface is pullovered and allowed to dry, it will be improved by burnishing. In the case of acid catalyst lacquers, polyurethane or polyester finishes, however, burnishing is essential after these surfaces have been flatted because pullovering is not possible.

There are two types of burnishing materials: pastes and creams. The pastes can be of fine, medium or coarse consistency and can be composed of pumice or rottenstone. The creams are for finishing off mirror gloss surfaces to remove the slight haze effect of the burnishing paste.

Cellulose-based lacquers that burnish

1. Nitrocellulose lacquer burnishes very easily with a cream or paste to a fully gloss finish.
2. Pre-catalysed lacquer burnishes well.
3. Acid-catalysed lacquer burnishes well.
4. Polyester lacquer is harder than nitrocellulose, yet will burnish easily, particularly with a power mop. Polyester is a special catalyst lacquer that *must* be burnished by power mop due to the make-up of the lacquer.

All lacquer must be completely dry and hard before burnishing. It must be 12 hours at least after the final application, or the surface film will tear up and become useless.

A burnishing paste is generally made by adding fine pumice or rottenstone to a standard (non-silicon) furniture cream with a little ammonia added. In today's trade houses, there are some excellent burnishing creams and pastes to suit every situation. Note that most burnishing creams contain carnauba waxes.

Methods of burnishing

Hand. Take a piece of mutton cloth, spread burnishing paste or fluid sufficient to cover the whole of the substrate and using slight pressure burnish all over using a circular motion, finally finishing with the direction of the grain in straight strokes.

Power Mop. Spread burnishing paste or fluid sufficient to cover the whole of the substrate and spread with a mutton cloth. Apply power mop at speeds between 2000/3000 rpm using a lambswool bonnet on the power head and burnish to a gloss finish. Finally finish off by hand using a clean piece of cloth. If a slight haze is visible, use a furniture cream to finish off.

These burnishing creams and waxes sometimes leave a "haze" which is not acceptable. This can be removed by using a standard furniture cream (non-silicon) or by adding french chalk to a standard reviver and rubbing on to the substrate vigorously, followed by a rub with a clean mutton cloth.

A haze remover

Mix the following ingredients together:
1 part methylated spirits
1 part white spirit
1 part raw linseed oil
1 part mild acetic acid (or white vinegar)
1 part soft water (rain or distilled)
2 parts french chalk

Shake well to mix before applying with a clean washed mutton cloth.

This haze remover *must not* be used on open-grained woods or the grain will be filled with a white deposit which is impossible to remove.

To avoid this, a pigment to suit the colour of the substrate can be added either to the burnishing cream or paste or to the haze remover.

Burnishing of a varnished surface

Good quality varnishes can be burnished. This comes as a surprise to most people as they think of varnish as being a surface coating that is brushed on and left alone, but this is not so. If a substrate has at least three or four coatings of an oil varnish (such as "yacht" or "exterior" which both dry by oxidation), these can be flatted down in the normal way and the final coat left to dry for at least seven days, after which burnishing can take place. No matter how carefully the brush application has been made, nibs will form. These must be removed by using 600 grade wet and dry abrasive paper using a little soap and water as a lubricant. Wipe off using a clean damp rag and proceed to burnish using a fine abrasive polish. The result can be surprising and can leave a fine smooth gloss finish which looks like glass. A power mop can be used but great care has to be taken not to "burn up" the surface. One great advantage of varnish is that it is a waterproof surface coating, and the burnished varnish will last much longer.

FLATTING

The student, or amateur wood finisher, usually spends little time in preparing the surface and yet the job is basically simple. There are a few easy and straightforward rules to be observed and care and attention must be paid to each stage of the process.

Any degree of flatting is determined in the first instance by "touching and looking", and this applies throughout the whole process of wood finishing.

In the case of a new, virgin surface, the wood must first be scraped using a cabinet scraper to remove the marks left by the machine planner as these are hideous if left untreated. The surface should then be sanded down using garnet abrasive papers. Faults such as cracks, chips and knots must be dealt with by using proper stoppers – that is, a stiff paste used for filling holes (usually applied with a putty knife) or shellac sticks, of varying colours. Make sure that you use the correct type – different stoppers are required for traditional or modern finishes. For example, beeswax stoppers must not be used under cellulose materials, but are ideal for shellac coatings. For large holes, it is sometimes advisable to make a "putty" of sawdust (of the wood concerned) mixed with a little thin animal glue, which, when dry can be sanded down to a smooth finish. Cellulose stoppers are designed for, and are compatible with, cellulose surface coatings.

The first part of the process on a virgin, or "in the white", piece of furniture in the workshop is to raise the grain by damping down with warm water. Don't get carried away by turning on the hose pipe or throwing a bucket of water over it! Simply damp down slightly with a piece of sponge or cloth and allow this to dry. When you run your fingers over the surface, you will feel that the grain has been raised. This has now to be sanded flat using a dry abrasive garnet paper 240 grade and dusted off.

After this first sanding, the stain must be applied, and you will have to decide what type. I prefer a water stain because it has several advantages over the other types available. First, it will slightly raise the grain again, although not as much as in the initial damping down stage, but it will really cover your wood evenly, penetrate well and will not fade as oil and spirits stains do.

Stains are best applied using a coloured cloth and rubbing well into the pores of the wood, then wiping off in the direct of the grain, *never*

A rubber sanding block used on a lacquer surface with water and soap as a lubricant and 400 grade wet or dry silicon carbide paper

across it. Leave the piece to dry out completely. If using traditional materials, a little ammonia added to the stain will help it to penetrate deeper into the grain, or if you are in a hard water area, use rain water or even add a few drops of good washing-up liquid to soften the water. Although this is not recommended if you are using cellulose-based modern finishing materials. When the stain has dried, sand down again, but this time more lightly, using Lubrisil 320 grade paper or garnet 240 grade abrasive papers.

Now you have to decide whether you want the grain left open or filled. If the latter, then this is the time to do it, either with a proprietary filler (there are many on the market), or by mixing your own. The "recipe" is to add enough plaster of paris to one pint of water to make a thin cream. To this add a little pigment to match your stain, 1 fl. oz. raw linseed oil, 1 fl. oz. shellac (bleached) and 2 fl. oz. methylated spirits. Mix all the ingredients well and apply the mixture to the wood using a piece of old hessian to force it into and across the grain. Wipe off as much as possible of the surface filler with clean hessian, allow to dry and sand down again in the direction of the grain. This is a dusty job so use a face mask! These stages may seem tedious, especially as you want to get on with the job, but time and trouble spent here will be amply rewarded in the final results. At this stage you recolour, using either the original stain or simply wiping over another thin spirit or oil stain and allowing it to dry out for 2-4 hours.

After the filling and sanding processes, there may be slight variations in the colour which may need touching in before the final application of a thin coat, or "tea-wash", of colour to blend in the variations.

"Touching in", or colouring, is filling in those areas around knots or "stopped" holes that show up lighter on the surface and need to be coloured out to make them blend in with the surrounding stains. To do this, make up a very thin mixture of methylated spirits with a very little "binder" such as bleached dewaxed shellac plus a little pigment, such as brown umber, burnt sienna, black, yellow ochre, venetian red or

115

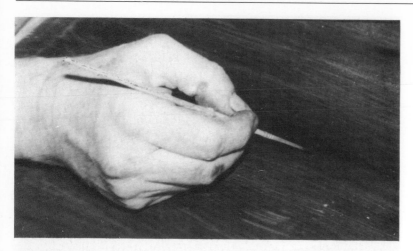

titanium white to be used as required, and apply the mixture to the blemishes with a pencil brush. To become a good "colourer" takes practice, a good eye and an artistic gift. An old egg box provides a useful container for the colours when touching in. When you have completed the touching in to your satisfaction, apply a "tea-wash" to the whole surface by fad or spray-gun to blend in the colour to the overall surface.

A "tea-wash" is a thin mixture of methylated spirits, a very little bleached shellac and a small amount of pigment so thin in consistency that it does not radically change the colour but simply blends in the touched-in areas with the background colour. If you intend to finish the work with lacquer, substitute thinners plus a little lacquer for the methylated spirits. There is no hard and fast rule, but it is essential that the staining and colouring should be done well at this stage because it is almost impossible to adjust once the first coating of a finishing film has been applied.

Now comes the final stage of the "flatting" technique. Whether you have chosen to french polish, varnish or lacquer the surface, you will find that the first application, when it has dried, has left it rough, full of nibs and showing any other visible faults on the surface. These have to be removed in such a way that no damage is caused to the surrounding film so that the next coat will flow over smoothly.

A nib is a minute particle of dust which has been trapped in the surface film and can be caused by:

1. Sanding dust, hairs and dust in the atmosphere from inside or outside the workshop.
2. Faulty rubbers, that is dirty or hard old rubbers that have collected dust.
3. Dust particles around the lips of tins. Wipe these first with a damp cloth before opening.
4. Dirty benches and floors. The whole area must be cleaned before applying any finishing material.
5. Dust falling from hanging lamps or flourescent tubes etc.
6. Small flying insects during the summer months.
7. Dust from dirty electric fans.

Touching in with shellac and pigments

Touching in with cellulose and pigments

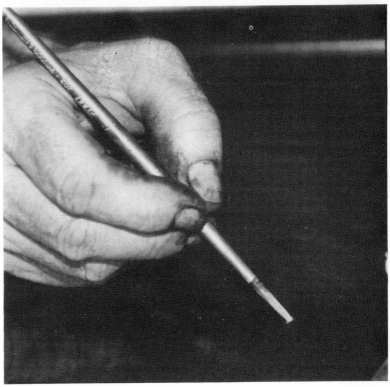

Keeping the work area scrupulously clean will minimise, although not totally eliminate, nibs. Use an old vaccuum cleaner both before commencing the work and after each dusty stage, and also keep any remaining dust particles down by lightly spraying the workshop with a water atomising sprayer (the type used for house-plants is ideal, as long as this is not overdone).

When the surface has these nibs, or any other fault, these can be removed by several methods (according to the type of finish).

Shellac or french polish. Use a waterproof silicon carbide abrasive paper, grade 400 or 600, with either raw linseed oil or mineral oil as a lubricant (never use water on a shellac surface or it will "bleach mark" white) or alternatively a dry silicon carbide paper such as Lubrisil 320 grade paper or, 000 or 0000 steel wool. Here again the steel wool could be used in conjunction with a lubricating oil if desired.

Oil resin varnish. Use either Lubrisil paper grade 320 dry, or better still a silicon carbide "wet and dry" paper grade 600, with rain water and soap as a lubricant.

Fine steel wool used in direction of grain to de-nib a French polished surface

Using Lubrisil 'dry' silicon carbide to de-nib a varnished surface

Flatting lacquers

Here again, use silicon carbide "wet and dry" grade 400 or 600 paper and rain water and soap, or white spirits as a lubricant. Never use oil on this surface or spraying faults can occur, such as cissing or "craters" due to the oily surface. It is the "sludge" produced in the flatting action, that is the combination of the abrasive paper, the lubricant and the surface film, that will be doing the actual job of flatting. All sludge should be wiped off with a clean damp cloth after use and the surface allowed to dry out.

Abrasive papers are best used in conjunction with a small cork or wooden sanding block with a ¼" felt base. Damage can occur by using a hard cork block without a felt base so care is required.

There are of course other faults that can appear on a film surface, such as blooming, blushing and crazing, but I have dealt with just one of the major irritations to the wood finisher – that of "nibs". You can now appreciate that care and effort carried out through the various processes of surface coating will bring about that "perfect finish".

A beezer

A beezer is a flatting device used in french polishing and is generally home made. It is mainly used by professional polishers to obtain a perfect flat finish on such large areas as grand piano lids, table tops etc. It consists of a length of ¼" thick felt, cut to a width of 2"-3", tightly rolled up and fastened by wire or nylon in the middle to hold it together. The whole thing is soaked in either linseed raw oil or any mineral oil and allowed to dry. The top is sealed by pouring on varnish and allowing to dry, while the other end is ground flat either by rubbing it on the side of a sandstone grinding wheel or rubbing well on a rough flagstone to a smooth and hard finish.

Wiping away the 'gunge' after de-nibbing a lacquer surface using wet or dry silicon carbide paper with soap and water.

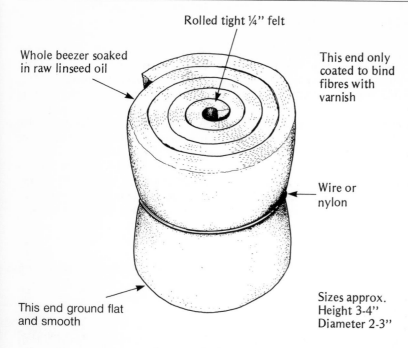

Rolled tight ¼" felt

Whole beezer soaked
in raw linseed oil

This end only
coated to bind
fibres with
varnish

*The 'Beezer' – used in flatting a French
polished surface*

Wire or
nylon

This end ground flat
and smooth

Sizes approx.
Height 3-4"
Diameter 2-3"

Storage when not in use
keep in sealed container

How to use the beezer

1. Spread the oil liberally on the french polished surface. The substrate *must* be well bodied up with a good depth of bone dry shellac.
2. Gently dust a little pumice powder onto the substrate, on the oil, and proceed to "scrub in" using the flat edge of the beezer, with a little pressure. Go round and round making sure that every inch of the substrate is covered. Do take care not to damage any corners.
3. When finished, wipe off any oil and pumice and leave the french polish dry.
4. Proceed to "body in" and thus finish off, leading to a perfect flat french polished finish.

CARE AND MAINTENANCE

Looking after your furniture

Today's furniture – made and finished with great skill by manufacturers – is soon covered by its owners with an ever-increasing assortment of creams, waxes, emulsions, oils and aerosol sprays. Beeswax, in particular, applied to the surface of furniture, in most cases does more harm than good.

The problem is deciding which oil, cream, aerosol or wax polish to apply to furniture. This is always the question that a professional polisher is asked, and the answer is that it all depends on the original finish. There are few finishes applied to furniture and they are basically: shellac or fresh polish, wax, oil, cellulose, varnish, or pigmented cellulose.

Shellac or french polish

French polish was applied to furniture and pianos from approximately 1800 up to the early thirties, and is still very popular. Most french polished surfaces need very little attention, although some need a little more depending on their usage. The procedure for cleaning is basically the same for most of the above furniture finishes, with the exception of oil and wax ones. Clean the surface first, if it is showing grime, by using a "reviver". This is a fluid mixture of five ingredients which, if rubbed on with a cloth will remove all the secondary built-up wax and grime lying on top of the original finish without doing any harm to the finish itself.

A reviver is made up by mixing equal parts by volume of raw linseed oil, methylated spirits, water, paraffin or turpentine and dilute acetic acid or white vinegar. Shake the ingredients together in a glass bottle and rub in liberally with a small piece of mutton cloth or cotton wool until the grime rolls off. In the case of extremely dirty furniture, such as greasy chair backs, add a couple of teaspoons of pumice powder to a pint of reviver to give it a little more "bite". After using the reviver, wipe down until dry and leave it for a little while. Then use a good branded furniture polish made by a specialist. Use a cream on a french polished surface with a full grain-filled gloss finish, but if the surface

121

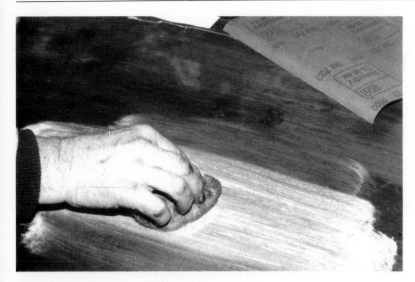

Using a 'reviver' fluid to clean a French polished surface

has open grain or is an antique then use a solid wax coloured polish such as a brown wax. In either case it is the burnishing action together with the wax or cream that gives you a shine or patina. In other words, 10% polish and 90% elbow grease!

A wax surface should not be sticky after polishing and a good test is to place your fingers lightly on the surface – if your fingers tend to stick then you have applied too much wax. Simply burnish again, preferably with mutton cloth as this has more "bite" than a yellow duster.

Wax finish

This is a surface which has had no other wood finishes applied but beeswax polish. It is often found on church and 17th century furniture, and can be cleaned and polished at the same time by using a coloured, good quality turpentine type (not paraffin) beeswax polish. Here again use sparingly and burnish with a lot of elbow grease. Do not use creams or aerosols on this type of surface finish.

Oil finish

This is mostly found used on teak, oak, and cedar (e.g. on garden furniture), and should simply be cleaned with turpentine and a little fine steel wool. Allow to dry and apply a coating of oil by brush, and burnish off dry. Raw linseed oil or teak oil are ideal for this type of finish. "Teak" oil is simply a blend of vegetable and mineral oils and can be used on other woods as well as teak.

Cellulose finishes

These also include pre-catalysed and acid-hardened lacquers, and polyurethane and polyester lacquers.

An oil finish – seen here on a font made by the author and oiled with raw linseed oil

Do not use wax polish or oil, simply wipe down with a damp rag washed in warm water with a little added white vinegar. Dry off using a clean piece of mutton cloth. There are certain aerosol sprays on the market which are plastic surface cleaners and are ideal for highly polished surfaces, such as polyester finishes, but apply the spray to the cloth (*not* the surface) and then burnish off dry.

Matt or semi-matt satin (dull) surfaces tend to become slightly shiny after the passage of time so apply light strokes in the direction of the grain using 0000 steel wool to "de-shine" the surface and then dust off. Never use a wax polish on a dull finish.

Varnish

All this finish requires, if the varnish is in good condition, is a wash down using warm water and soap or detergent. Allow to dry and then burnish with a clean mutton cloth and a little wax furniture polish. On no account use aerosols or oil.

Pigmented finishes

These are often the "white" or "cream" finishes found on modern bedroom furniture which can be cleaned by using a special "Melamine" cream which looks like milk, or simply by wiping down, using a muslin cloth with a little soap and water. Beware of harsh cleaning creams and never use harsh cleaning powders. Dry with a clean muslin cloth to remove any streaks.

It is a good plan to have a small service kit for the home, to be used for furniture only. This should be made up of a tin or plastic box containing:
1. A reviver kept in a bottle for cleaning wood surfaces.
2. Mutton cloth (well-washed) to be used for all polishing purposes.
3. A piece of fine steel wool (000 or 0000 grades).
4. A soft brush (used to dust into corners).
5. An old toothbrush (used to clean out mouldings and carvings).
6. Wadding or cotton wool (used with general cleaning).
7. Light brown furniture polish.
8. Furniture cream.
9. Anti-woodworm fluid and anti-woodworm wax polish.

Precautions

Do not use furniture cream on open-grained finishes. Use the correct "colour" polish to match as nearly as possible the wood in question.

Aerosol polishes and silicones

These are the new breed of wax polishes which have become very popular during recent years. Such small canisters of pressurized liquid polish must be used with care. Many polishers hate them, but I must admit that they have their uses in wood-finishing.

A surface on which other aerosols have been used must first be cleaned before another brand of polish is applied, as they may not be compatible. Clean off the old surface wax content and allow to dry before using (sparingly) a little aerosol spray polish. Spray this onto the cloth first and then apply this to the surface and burnish. Take care and keep the following points in mind:

1. Never use aerosol polishes near a naked flame (open fire or gas fire).
2. Keep good ventilation while using aerosols.
3. Keep away from children and pets.
4. Store in a cool dark place – never in the sun.
5. Use sparingly.

Silicone polishes

Silicones are produced chemically and are very complex in structure. When they are added to furniture polish they produce an easy-gloss, water-resistant finish. There are a great many on the market today and most of them come in the form of aerosols. A quick spray of the polish onto a substrate followed by a wipe down with a lint-free cloth produces an easy shine, and these types of polish are ideal for the less expensive furniture with foil-covered substrates – for example printed finishes, and also for commercial furniture of the type found in hotels, restaurants etc. They are not recommended, however, for cellulose finishes, because there is a tendency for them to build up a surface film, nor for matt finished surfaces. They should not be used on antique furniture of any kind. Where their use is suitable, they should be used sparingly.

Central heating

Central heating can be a menace to any item of wood, whether it be furniture or joinery. Wood is a natural hygroscopic substance – in warm dry conditions it gives up moisture and in damp conditions it absorbs it – so a happy balance has to be achieved. Central heating is responsible for more damage to old furniture and antiques than any other single factor – even the passage of time. I have been in houses where valuable furniture was placed directly in front of radiators, causing cracking, warping and damage to the surface finish.

Preventing damage is easier than curing it, and by following a few simple guidelines you can help your furniture and central heating to live together in harmony.

1. Install a humidifier if a great deal of quality furniture is involved.
2. If no humidifier is available, place a shallow bowl of clean water under pianos-antiques etc.
3. If at all possible, allow some outside air to enter the room area each day.

125

4. Never place furniture (new or old) in front of radiators.
5. Treat the dry unfinished parts of furniture (such as the backs and under the bottom sections) with a 50% mixture of turpentine and raw linseed oil.
6. Keep older furniture well wax polished.
7. Inspect furniture regularly, particularly any pieces which are veneered. If the veneers are showing signs of cracking, remove the furniture to a cooler place in the house, perhaps near an outside door or in a hall where there is no radiator. Leave it there until the furniture has absorbed moisture and is quickly restored to its original state.

WOOD EATERS

Everyone knows how to identify woodworm in furniture – by the appearance of the flight-holes in the wood and by the tell-tale deposit of fine whitish powder found on the carpet under the furniture. This is "frass" – the excrement of the grubs. The discovery is common, and disturbing to the owners, but the problem can be treated and the unwanted guests evicted very simply. If dealt with in time, very little harm will have been done to your furniture. Most antique furniture had at some time been infected by wood eaters, yet has survived.

These wood-eating insects fall into two groups:

1. Insects that inhabit joinery and carpentry (in buildings); for example, the death-watch beetle (xestobium rufovillosum), the powder post beetle (lyctus) and the house longhorn beetle (hylotrupes bajulus).

2. Insects that inhabit furniture; for example the common furniture beetle (anobium punctatum).

The latter is public enemy No. 1 to wooden furniture! It is helpful to understand a little about the life-cycle of this insect. The breeding season starts in July/August when the newly-wed Mr. and Mrs. Anobium Punctatum set up home in some warm, undisturbed and untreated corner of your sideboard and immediately start a large family. The eggs develop into grubs about ¼" long who then spend the next three years eating into your sideboard before finally becoming fully-grown beetles and flying off in early summer to start all over again on your dressing-table!

Such woods as oak, pine, mahogany, boxwood, and walnut provide suitable homes for these insects. However, some woods have a built-in chemical immunity to wood-eating insects, such as burmese teak, cedar and rosewood. These are safe but the others are not, even hard bamboo is as good as meat and two veg. to a woodworm beetle grub! Any furniture which has plywood in its construction is liable to woodworm infestation and if any flight holes are visible it is a waste of time and effort to try and eradicate the worm. Simply remove the whole piece and replace it with new. Soft plywood to a grub is the yorkshire pudding that goes with the meat and two veg!

Prevention is always better than cure, so once a year around spring-cleaning time I would suggest the following procedure:

1. Empty out any drawers or cupboards and then turn the piece upside

A death watch beetle

A house longhorn beetle

down and apply anti-woodworm fluid by brush to all bare unfinished rough areas including the backs, legs and inside the backs of drawers and allow to dry out. Most woodworm fluids are now low-odour – check when you buy.

2. Clean outside and apply an anti-woodworm wax polish – a special blend of waxes and anti-woodworm fluids. An ideal one is produced by a nationally known anti-woodworm company.

Furniture which is badly infested with worm

Apply anti-woodworm fluid all over the item including the bottoms of the legs, and, if possible use an injector bottle to help penetrate deeper into the wood. Wrap the whole item up in a thin plastic sheet like a parcel and leave for 24 hours – this will act like a fumigation chamber. Remove the item after 24 hours and wax polish all over using the anti-woodworm polish.

A powder post beetle

An adult anobium punctatum (common furniture beetle)

If any legs are badly infected, simply stand the legs in tins which have been half filled with anti-woodworm fluid and leave overnight. The fibre of the wood will draw up the fluid into the legs.

Paraffin oil, turpentine oil and white spirits with a little added creosote can also be used to treat the backs of items, but the odour may not be acceptable to some people. It is interesting that turpentine was used for hundreds of years by ship's carpenters on H.M. warships – even they had trouble with the wood-eaters!

Should the wood be so badly affected as to be structurally unsafe then expert replacement of the parts concerned will probably be necessary.

Ironically the scourge of the twentieth century, pollution, has an odd

A pupa anobium punctatum in cell

A larva of anobium punctatum which spends three years boring through wood

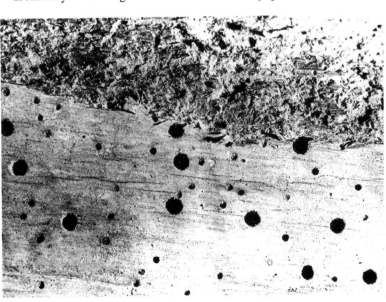

Timber beams showing evidence of heavy infestations of death watch beetles and common furniture beetles

Evidence of woodworm on the underside of softwood floorboards

A 'Rentokil' operator spraying anti-woodworm fluid into floorboards and joists

beneficial side-effect. It helps to keep down the menace of woodworm in areas where there is heavy traffic or industry. In country areas, like Devon and Cornwall, woodworm is endemic and thriving.

There are, however, other wood-eaters called termites or white ants, mainly found in tropical parts of the globe. Any one who has lived in these parts will know full well that not only do they eat furniture but very quickly your home as well!

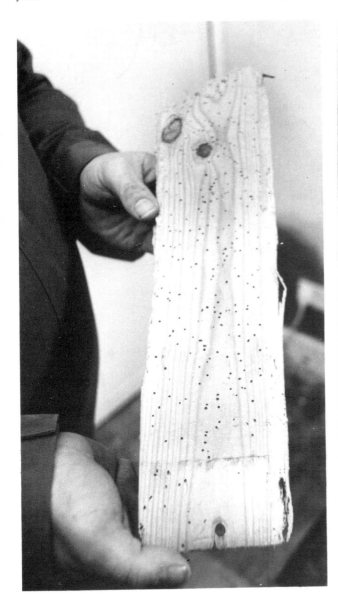

FLOOR POLISHING

There are many problems that can be encountered when finishing a wooden floor. It is no use applying a wood finish to a floor only to see in a few weeks time that it has become badly scratched, scoured and stained. The main problems, therefore, are durability of the surface coating and maintenance. Both of these go hand in hand with each other.

One of the main hazards faced by a finished wooden floor is the human being! The male of the species scours it with heavy work boots or garden shoes, the female hammers hundreds of tiny dents into it with the steel tips of her high-heeled shoes. It would take a whole book to list the other things which they, their offspring and their pets can do to the floor!

In the past every conceivable type of wooden floor-finishing surface coating has been used from french polish to varnish, cellulose or polyurethane. Yet every coated finish will in time wear away and the whole process of recoating has to be undergone. Manufacturers have for years been trying to find the ideal material to brush or spray on to wood which will outlast anything else on the market, and yet be easy to service or maintain. Many products are now available which require a minimum of care to keep them looking good.

Refurbishing an old floor (hard or softwood)

1. In any building more than 25 years old, check any floor area for wood-eating insects – particularly the common furniture beetle (woodworm), or if the floor substrate is oak – the deathwatch beetle and others. Remove one floorboard in four and spray or brush on an anti-woodworm fluid, or if "fungus" is visible – a special dry or wet rot liquid. Make sure that all exposed wood surfaces are treated and that the undersides of the floorboards are also checked, and treated if required. Anti-woodworm fluids normally have a very low odour, but it is better to carry out this work during a day when you can ensure maximum ventilation. Face masks should also be worn when applying these fluids. This work is well worth the effort and time spent on it, since you will have the peace of mind of knowing that these areas have been cleared of any pest infestation.

2. Carry out any minor repairs that are needed, such as a loose or "floating" joist.
3. Position and nail down the floorboards.
4. Check for, and deal with, any loose floorboards.
5. Nail punch all nail heads just below the surface of the boards.
6. Check for gaps – do not use any patent stoppers for this as they will work out very quickly as people walk on the floorboards. Simply make wooden wedged fillets and hammer them home tightly.
7. If the floor has had a surface finish, remove it by chemical stripping with a water-washable paint stripper. This must be done during a good dry day when windows and doors can be left open, as most strippers contain methylene chloride and some ammonia. Face masks should also be worn during this operation. When all traces of paint, varnish etc. have been removed, wash all over with clean water (with a very little detergent) and leave to dry out. Washing with water will clean down the surface, raise the grain, and neutralize the chemical stripper.
8. The floor should now be sanded using a belt sander, for a large floor surface, or an orbital sander. The former is preferable. Remove any protruding knots by planing or rasping down flat, followed by resanding. Use a face mask to avoid inhaling the dust which will be raised.
9. Use a vacuum cleaner to remove all traces of dust from the floor.
10. The substrate is now ready for refinishing. Most old floorboards, in spite of stripping and sanding, need a little stain, and it is better to use a water stain rather than an oil medium type. The advantages of a water stain on a floor are good penetration, no odour, and compatibility with any type of wood finish.

Finishes

Decision time has now been reached on the kind of surface finish required. The choice is as follows.

1. Hard drying floor varnishes

These are special varnishes made from synthetic resins – lacquers, polyurethanes etc, that simply brush on. These, with multiple coatings, give a high-build gloss or satin surface film which is generally oil, water, acid, alkaline and "children" resistant.

Advantages of the hard-drying surface coatings

1. They are very easy to apply either by brush or spray-gun.
2. They are quick-drying – approximately 2-6 hours at 65°F.
3. They are resistant to most household hazards.
4. No skill is required to apply them.
5. They can be obtained clear, satin or coloured, and ready to use from the tin.

133

Disadvantages of the hard-drying surface coatings

1. They can scratch and chip.
2. They must be maintained with further applications of surface coating.
3. They take a fair while to dry out, rendering the room out-of-bounds for a time.
4. They should not be used on teak or cedar woods.
5. Odours from these surface coatings can be very unpleasant, particularly polyurethane finishes.

2. Special traditional floor finishes – oil or wax

Special oils such as cedar oil, and "traffic waxes" made from paraffin waxes (anti-slip) are ideal for all quality hardwoods and softwoods. Simply apply by rag and polish with an electric floor polisher or by hand. Various "coloured" waxes are available for floors as well as "natural".

Advantages of traditional floor oil finishes

1. They are very easy to apply.
2. They can be walked on immediately.
3. They act as a deterrent against wood-eating pest infestation.
4. All damages, scratches etc. can be simply oiled out with further applications.

Disadvantages of traditional floor oil finishes

1. There is an odour with some oils that some people find unpleasant.
2. Only a satin finish can be achieved.
3. They require hand application.
4. They are only available in clear oils.

Advantages of special traditional floor wax polishes

1. They are anti-slip.
2. They are obtainable in coloured waxes.
3. They can be mechanically buffed.
4. The wax acts as an anti-woodworm deterrent.
5. They fill up any small cracks or holes.
6. They clean and polish at the same time.
7. They can be walked on immediately after polishing.

Disadvantages of special traditional floor wax polishes

1. They require constant servicing.
2. Some people find the odour from the paraffin-based wax polish unpleasant.

DISTRESSING

To "distress" in wood finishing means to simulate old, well-worn wood surface finishes. It is to imitate the effects on the wood which the passage of time would have caused. This technique of imitating wear and tear could be called "faking", but somehow this word has a rather disturbing note to it. I prefer the term distress which gives a rather more dignified value to the work involved. A good distressed finish does not rely simply on the finish – work must also be carried out on the substrate before any distressing of the finish can be contemplated.

Distressing of the wood or substrate

This is carried out by the use of woodworking hand tools such as carving tools or gouge chisels, an adze (this is for large carpentry work such as beams, planks etc.), a rasp, a sharp pointed bladed knife (stanley type).

An example of distressing, illustrated, shows a new wooden beam that has been fitted to a room full of old oak beams and the new wood stands out like a rape seed flower in a field of corn. Distressing of the new wood is essential to blend it in with the old.

Procedure for distressing new wood

1. Cut into all sharp corners with chisels to remove the straight lines left by the power sawing machine.
2. Rasp out all machine markings, with and across the grain.
3. Cut in shakes and splits at random, using the pointed knife or chisels.
4. Cut out one or two knots, leaving the actual knot protruding.
5. Using a curved or gouge carving chisel, hand tool the flat areas so that there are no actual plain sawn areas left visible.
6. Cut false mortices at specified random positions, and fit wooden pegs cut off at varying lengths – these can be very effective if used carefully.
7. Simulate woodworm holes by using a 1/16th" drill to bore clusters of holes.

Pinewood distressed to resemble oak, in harmony with the original oak beams

Study old beams etc., particularly any which you are aiming to match. Then try to simulate the ageing and detail as nearly as possible. One word of warning – it is very easy to get carried away and produce an over-simulated effect, whilst it is also just as easy to under-work an effect. A happy balance has to be achieved.

Distressing the finish

After the work on the wood substrate has been carried out to your satisfaction, the finish is of paramount importance. It is no use having an artistic, distressed piece of wood if it is ruined by a simple coating of dark oak varnish and left at that. The distressed substrate must therefore be coloured and finished with a suitable surface coating. This depends on the actual item being distressed, furniture or carpentry, and also whether it is for interior or exterior use. The finish coating can be wax, oil, shellac, cellulose or varnish and a good spirit-based colouring pigment should be used. The depth of the finishing coating should be substantial, and any of the normal methods of application – such as fad, rubber, mop, brush or even spray-gun can be used. The surface coating must then be allowed to dry completely before the actual distressing can commence.

Close-up of distressed pinewood, resembling old oak

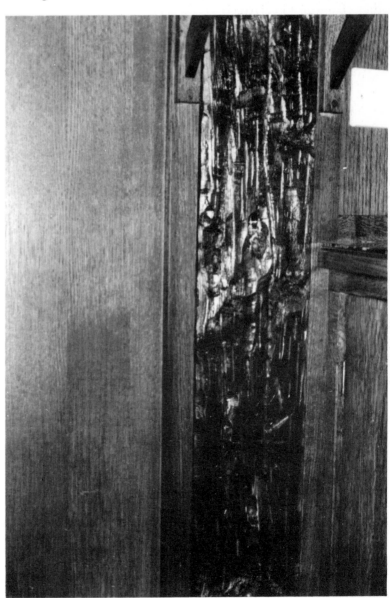

Various methods of distressing a finish

When distressing reproduction furniture, a lump of loose iron chain is ideal to simulate old markings. This is achieved by bumping down hard on the finish using the chain in a loose lump – some operators dip the chain first in black/brown umber pigment to give added effect. Another known way of simulating markings is to use a lump of brick or stone with sharp corners and to simply dent the surface by pressing down hard.

Burn marks can be produced easily by pre-heating the bottom of a small empty tin – a bean tin is a good size – by holding it over a naked flame until it is very hot. Then simply place it on the finished surface. Smaller burn marks can be produced with other objects, such as the tip of an old screwdriver, similarly heated up and applied.

Ink stains which often appear on genuine old desks can be simulated by applying black pigment mixed with shellac to the underside of a small bottle and gently pressing down on the finish leaving a ring of pigment to resemble ink.

Again, as with the distressing of the substrate, do not overdo the distressing of the finish. One or two marks are usually enough.

All genuine old surfaces have a dull finish, so to remove the gloss effect of new polish during finishing, mix pumice powder with a good wax polish and rub well in. Fine steel wool used with furniture wax polish has the same effect.

On reproduction work to create a simulated "age" effect on new raw corners, carvings and mouldings, use a "gunge" mixture of black and brown umber pigments mixed with shellac. Apply it by mop to the large surfaces and fine brush into the carvings and mouldings. While it is still wet drop a little pumice powder over the surfaces. When dry the effect is of a dusty antique finish which can then be waxed and dulled as the situation requires.

"Touching-up" or "brush-distressing" is another technique used to age and add character. Simply apply irregular fine brush lines with a pencil brush using a mixture of brown umber and black pigments mixed with shellac. The lines should be faint and painted both along and across the grain at random. Again – don't overdo it!

Scratches are the easiest of the distressing methods to achieve. Simply scratch the polished surface using a nail or bradawl. The cavities will show up white and these should be aged by applying a mixture of brown umber and shellac directly into the scratch with a pencil brush.

"Splattering" is another way of giving a simulated appearance of age to a new surface and is now commonly used in finishing reproduction furniture. The finish, if properly carried out, gives a very pleasing effect and helps to tone down and mellow furniture made by machinery. The method can also be used in antique restoration but has to be done very carefully as it is easy for the operator to get carried away and over-do "the spots". There are three main ways of "splattering" which it is best to try out first on a spare piece of hardboard until you achieve the effect you want. In all three cases, first mix the pigment of your choice to a creamy consistency with cellulose thinners and a little matt

The restoration of the top section of Stuart period furniture – new English oak distressed to blend in with the original

lacquer to act as a binder and strain the mixture through a metal sieve or nylon stocking.

The first method is to take a piece of wood (about 10″ x 2″ x 1″) and place it on the item of furniture close to the area which you wish to splatter. Dip a 1″ long-haired used bristle paint brush into the mixture of pigment and knock the ferrule of the brush onto the wood which will cause the pigmented mixture to spot or spit onto the surface.

The second method is to simply take the paint brush loaded with the mixture and flick the tips of the bristles causing the mixture to splatter across the surface. This method is a little messy, so remember to warn anyone in the work area to stand well clear!

The best and easiest method is to use a quality spray-gun, such as the "Devilbiss Gravity Feed", which has an in-built attachment to give a fully controlled splatter effect, including the frequency of the spots.

A "limed finish" is not strictly speaking a distressed finish, but an effect which became popular many years ago and which is now enjoying a come-back. It is mainly used on re-production furniture and panelling. Liming is a method of producing a very pleasing effect by rubbing a white filler into the grain of any open-grained woods such as oak, elm, ash etc, and polishing over with a clear polish. Traditional polishers used unslaked lime to achieve this effect, but that is a thing of the past.

To produce a limed finish:
1. Damp down the substrate to raise the grain.
2. Using a metal wire brush, scrub out heavily in the direction of the grain – the object is to remove all soft tissue fibres of the grain or simply to open up the grain more.
3. Slightly sand down using 240 grade abrasive garnet papers.
4. Dust down with a dusting brush to clear out the waste.

5. Apply white liming filler polish across the grain of the wood and wipe off. When dry after, say, six hours or more, slightly sand down in the direction of the grain.

6. Apply a few coatings of a "white" french polish by rubber simply to seal in the liming polish. Leave to dry hard for between 6-12 hours.

After the wire brushing stage, the substrate can, if required, be stained. A "water-type" stain must be used. Some very pleasing effects can be produced by using white filler lime polish in the grain on stained wood.

POWERED MACHINES

All workshops nowadays – large or small – use powered wood-finishing equipment in some form or another. Most of these machines are sold in ever-increasing quantities: some are good, some are not so good, and it is a matter of choosing a machine that suits the job in hand and not a price. The advertised lists of these machines are endless, yet the basic principles of sanding and polishing wood remain the same. The traditional sanding action of using a cork block in conjunction with an appropriate abrasive paper used in the direction of the grain is by far the best way of finishing wood, so any machine that can simulate this action is by far the best one to obtain and use.

It is interesting that powered machines have entirely taken over the woodworking trades – machines that will saw, dovetail, make mortice and tenons, rebate mould and so on. Some machines are even computerised. It will, alas, not be long before hand tools are museum pieces although fortunately this is not entirely so with woodfinishing. True, there are machines that prepare wood (the sanding machines) and some actually apply finishing coatings, but the emphasis is still on the side of "hand-control" power machines and I cannot see it changing in spite of modern technology.

Sanding or preparation machines

There are three basic types, all hand-held and electrically powered.

1. The orbital sanding machine

This is a machine with a rectangular-based thick pad which is used in conjunction with various sanding abrasive papers and the powered action is front, side and backward motion at high speed. The power is approximately 250-300 watts and the speed of these machines can be 6000-24000 rpm – the faster the action the better the finish. They are ideal for very large surfaces, panels etc., and very little effort is required in using them. You must simply hold on and not let go! They produce a fine smooth finish provided the correct grades of abrasive papers are used. To finish off using this type of sander, simply follow

141

the direction of the grain. Caution is required on edges of the sub-strates or damage can occur. It is advisable to wear a face dust mask when using these machines.

The orbital sander, however, has one fault. As the action of the machine orbits and reciprocates, it causes the formation of "whorls" or cross-cutting circles at the end of each powered stroke action. This can be undesirable for quality finishing work and the answer to this problem is to finish off by the hand method using 240 grade garnet abrasive papers with a cork block.

2. The "belt" sanding machine

The advantage of this machine over the orbital sander is that it does not orbit, that is provided that the operator keeps the machine in the direc-

Sanding action across the grain, with a powered orbital sanding machine with dust collecting bag

Finishing off in the direction of the grain

tion of the grain, and the sanding action, with a continuous belt of abrasive paper will never produce whorls on the substrate. It is ideal for all cabinet work, joinery and basic carpentry.

A belt-sanding machine can be used for sanding chamfers, edges, curves etc. The better quality machines are "electronic", with a varying speed control which allows the machine to be adjusted even to delicate veneer work. Here again, the best sander has a built-in extraction bag to keep dust to a minimum, but in this age of health and safety-consciousness, it is desirable to wear a dust mask when using these machines in spite of dust-bag extraction.

3. The rotary disc sander

This hand-powered machine is usually used on rough wood where the problem of cross grain cutting is of no importance, such as sanding down pinework prior to painting. The discs are of varying abrasive grades and simply rotate on a fixed rubber backing pad. Two disadvantages of this type of rotary sanding action is the dust problem and the cross circle whorls that the sanding discs produce. They can also be used for sanding or stripping paint from doors, window-sills etc. Various attachments are manufactured for this popular power unit, and these have their uses for the wood finisher. These rotary disc sanders should never be used on substrates that will be clear surface coated or for sanding veneered surfaces.

Coating machines

These machines can apply, mechanically, surface coatings to any flat substrate such as blockboard, chipboard, solid wood (hard or soft), Multiple Density Fibre (MDF) Board, plywood, veneers etc. The surface coatings can be cellulose and other synthetic lacquers (clear or pigmented), sealers and base coats. These machines cost many thousands of pounds and are essential for large manufacturers of furniture such as pianos, wardrobes, tables, kitchen fittings etc. They require, however, experienced operators both for their use and maintenance.

The main advantages in using surface coating machines are:
1. Great ease of area application to the various substrates.
2. An accurate, controlled uniform thickness of coating material.
3. A great saving of surface coating (unlike conventional spray application when there is "overspray" wastage).
4. Savings on labour – an economical advantage not to be ignored by large concerns.
5. Fewer fire and health hazards.
6. Fewer surface film faults.

Curtain coating machine

One of the most popular and effective machines that applies wood finishing materials is the curtain coating machine. This is a device that passes a substrate through a flowing "trough" of coating material on a conveyor. There is no wastage of costly materials, except of the solvents through evaporation. A continuous feed conveyor belt with substrates, in conjunction with a continuous "curtain" of finishing fluids, maintains a controlled rapid-flowing production line of surface coating. The main precautions for perfect application of coating material is the viscosity of the material and temperature control. These must be accurately maintained at all times.

A typical finishing manufacturer's instructions for curtain coating machine operators reads: "Apply by curtain coater 20 gm per ft^2 (200 gm per m^2) of matt or gloss pigments, polyester etc." The curtain coater is the ideal machine where a heavy film coating is required to a substrate, such as for polyester application.

Roller coating machine

This is another coating machine that applies a surface coating to any flat substrate by means of two rollers, one mounted above the other (like a mangle). When rotated mechanically, the top roller "anti-clockwise" and the bottom one "clockwise", the substrate passes through the gap between them, which can be adjusted to varying depths. Like the curtain coater a trough above the top roller cascades the surface coating liquid onto the top roller and discharges the coating of, say, an acid catalysed lacquer onto the substrate as it passes below.

The surface must be perfectly flat or an uneven amount of lacquer thickness will result – the roller must make contact with the substrate. Again, like the curtain coater, the correct viscosity and temperature control are very important for the efficient operation of the machine.

Polishing machines

Burnishing powered polishing machines

Various types of hand-held, rotating polishing or burnishing machines are available. They use a rubber base-plate with a lambswool bonnet tied to it. This cuts down the time and effort required when the operation is carried out by hand. Modern wood surface coatings also require a certain amount of heat, generated by friction, which is impossible to achieve by hand motion. Thus, a powered polisher in conjunction with varying grades of burnishing creams or pastes will produce an excellent gloss finish. The better quality rotating burnishing machines have speeds up to 3000 rpm, and most machines have varying speeds. Great care is required not to burn into the surface film and thus render the film useless, particularly when burnishing varnishes.

A powered polishing machine, with a lambswool bonnet, burnishing a gloss nitrocellulose finish

Specialised power edge mop polishing machines

Nitrocellulose, polyester and acid-hardened surface coatings can also be burnished using edge mops. These mops are built up of rotating laminated discs of linen or wool with spacers between. The discs are "puckered" to produce air flow. This minimises the heat caused by friction when in rotation of speeds of 2000 rpm or more. Normally these edge mops are fixed like a large "grinding machine" with two rotating mops on each side of a centralised powered motor, but there are portable edge mops for burnishing. Felt or nylon belts can be used in conjunction with a belt sander, but with a burnishing action. These machines can also be adapted to give "matt" finishes, as well as shiny gloss finishes, by using cutting compounds.

Care is again required in using the edge mops, as damage to the surface coating can easily be sustained due to frictional heat.

SUPPLIERS OF MATERIALS

John Myland Ltd., (inc. Gedge & Co.)
80, Norwood High Street,
London SE27 9NW
(Materials of all kinds for the polishing trade)

W.S. Jenkins & Co. Ltd.,
Jeco Works,
Tariff Road,
Tottenham,
London N17 0EN
(Specialist in modern finishing materials – cellulose, pre-cat and A/C
lacquers, melamine finishes, stains, sealers etc.)

E. Parson and Sons Ltd.,
Blackfriars Road,
Nailsea,
Bristol BS19 2BO
(Manufacturers of stains, dyes, varnishes etc.)

English Abrasives Ltd.,
P.O. Box 85,
Marsh Lane,
London N17 0XA
(Manufacturers of all types of abrasive papers)

Fiddes and Son Ltd.,
Trade Street,
Cardiff,
Wales
(Materials of all kinds for the polishing trade)

L.G. Wilkinson Ltd.,
Jenkins Lane,
Barking,
Essex IG11 0AB
(Specialists in modern wood finishing surface coatings – cellulose, pre-
cat and A/C lacquers, polyester and polyurethane lacquers etc.)

146

J.W. Bollom & Co. Ltd.,
Bromel Paint Mills,
Croydon Road,
Elmers End,
Beckenham,
Kent BR3 4BL
(Specialists in pigmented and woodfinishes of all kinds spray guns and accessories etc.)

The Devilbiss Co. Ltd.,
Ringwood Road,
Bournemouth BH11 9LH
(Manufacturers of quality spray gun equipment and compressors)

Clarke Group,
Lower Clapton Road,
London E5 0QR
(Suppliers of spray gun equipment and compressors)

Sterling Roncraft,
Chapeltown,
Sheffield S30 4YP
(Manufacturers of oil stains and varnishes etc.)

Evode Ltd.,
Common Road,
Stafford, ST16 3EH
(Manufacturers of water stains, varnishes and adhesives)

Cuprinol Ltd.,
Adderwell,
Frome,
Somerset BA11 1NL
(Manufacturers of exterior wood preservatives)

Rentokil Ltd.,
218 London Road,
East Grinstead,
West Sussex RH19 1HF
(Major manufacturers of wood pest control, dry and wet rot materials and specialist services for pest control in buildings)

Sonneborn & Rieck Ltd.,
91-95, Peregrine Road,
Hainault,
Ilford,
Essex
(Manufacturers of specialist lacquers, french polishes etc.)

Wilcot (Decorative Products) Ltd.,
Alexendra Park,
Fishponds,
Bristol BS16 2BQ
Trade Mark: "NITROMORS"
(Paint, emulsion, french polish, lacquer, chemical strippers)

R. Mould Ltd.,
Roundways,
West Howe Industrial Estate,
Elliott Road,
Bournemouth,
Dorset BA11 8JJ
(Cotton fibres, wadding, upholsteries accessories)

West Bourne Cleaning Supplies Ltd.,
99/101, Cheriton High Street,
Folkestone,
Kent CT19 4HE
(Paper wipers, tissues and hygiene materials)

INDEX

Abrasives 23
Abrasive coated materials 25
Abrasive papers 25
Acetate 108
Acids and alkalis 64
Acid catalysed lacquers 95
Acid finish 87
Alcohol 91, 92
Alkaline 64
Alkyd resins 77
Aluminium oxide 25
Ammonia .880 64
Antique reviver 89
Anti-woodworm fluids 131

Barrier creams 10
Beeswax 121
Beezer 119, 120 17, 87
Bleaching wood 33
Blockboard 13
Blooming 106
Bodying-in 86
Boiled Linseed oil 79
Broodlac 73
Brushes 17
Brown umber and burnt umber 54
Button polish 74
Burnishing 108, 112

Cabinet scraper 15, 16
Cappings 28
Caustic soda 43
Carnauba wax 30
Cellulose lacquers 91
Chemical stains 60
Chemical stripping 40
Chipboard 14
Cissing 103

Cotton rags 21
Creosote oil 129
Curtain coating machine 143

Death watch beetle 129
Dermatitis 9
Dewaxed shellac 32
Dilute sulphuric acid 87
Distressing 135, 139
Dry back spray booth 107
Dust 7, 8
Dyes 55

Early Greeks 1
Easters 46
Egyptians 1
Electric floor polishers 134
Emery papers 26
Extractor fans 8
Eye goggles 34
Extra pale polish 74

Fad 82
Face masks 94
Fillers (grain) 45
Fire extinguishers 6
Fire hazards 6
Finishing off (spiriting) 87
Fitch 20
Flame retardant intumescent varnish 77
Flash point 4
Flatting 119
Floor polishing 132
Flow cup No.4 96
French polishes 2, 74, 85
Fuming 64

Garnet abrasive papers 25

Garnet french polish 74
Glass paper 23
Gloss lacquers – various 90
Gloves 34
Goggles 8, 34
Gold leaf 2, 17
Grass brush 34
Gravity feed spray guns 98-99
Gum arabic 1, 76
Gum copal 76
Gum turpentine 80

Hand barrier cream 10
Hazards 6, 7
Haze removers 112
Health and safety 61, 101
Hessian 21
Host trees 74
Hot spray lacquer 97
House longhorn beetle 128
Hydrogen peroxide 34

In the white 114
Irritants 7
Isocyanate fumes 94

Jam stopper 50
Japan wax 31
Joinery 2

Keytones 46
Knots 50
Knotting 75

Lac beetle 73
Lac wax 32
Laccifer lacca 1, 73
Lacquers – various 90
Lambswool bonnet 111
Lime finish 139
Linseed oil (Raw) 79
Lubrisil 25
Lye 43

Marine varnish (yacht) 81
Matt lacquer 124
M.D.F. board 13, 143
Melamine 91
Methylated spirits 84, 108, 112
Methylene chloride 40
Microporous varnish 78

Mineral oil 79, 84
Modern wood finishing 90
Mops 18
Mutton cloth 112

Naptha stains 68
Neutralize 36
Nibs 105
Nitrocellulose lacquer 38, 91
Non-grain-raising stains 69
Non-reversible 38

Oak 11
Oil bound fillers 45
Oil stains 56
Orbital sanders 141
Oxalic acid 34
Ozokerite wax 32

Pale french polish 74
Paper towels/cloths 22
Paraffin wax 31
Piano finish 88
Pigments 54, 124
Plywood 12
Polyester lacquer 73
Polyurethans lacquer 73
Polyurethans varnish 77
Power polishing machines 112, 141
Pre-catalysed lacquer 91
Pullover fluids 108, 109
Pumice powder 26

Quills 17

Rags 21, 22
Raw linseed oil 84
Resin bound filler 45
Resin oil varnish 77, 118
Reversible finishes 37
Reviver 121
Roller coating machine 144
Rottenstone 26
Roof shingles 68
Rubbers 83, 86

Sanding 114
Scrubbing brush 34
Sealers 52
Seed lac 74
Shellac 74

Shellac sealer 75
Skin complaints 9
Soap 119
Spirit stains 58
Spirit varnish 78
Spray booths 197
Spray guns 9, 95
Stains 53
Steel wool 26
Stoppers 114
Stripping 40
Substrates 11, 13, 46
Suction pressure feed guns 98
Synthetic varnishes 76

Tak rags 22
Tannic acid 62
Tea wash 55, 116
Teak oil 80
Timber preserving fluids 68
Thinners 46
Toxic chemicals – fumes 7
Touching in (up) 75, 115
Treatise of japanning 1, 76
Turpentine 80

Ultra violet rays 94
Upholsterers wadding 22
Urea formaldehyde 91

Van Dyke brown 66
Varnish 67, 77
Vegetable oils 84
Veneers 11
Vienna chalk 26
Viscosity testing 95

Wadding 22, 82
Washed mutton cloth 21
Water stains 66
Wax finish 1, 122
White french polish 85
White spirit 80
Wire brushes 21
Wire wool 26
Wood eaters 129
Wood grain filler 45
Wood preserving stains 68
Wood substrates 11
Wood worm 129
Woodworm flight holes 50, 129
Wooden floors 133

Xycol 46

Yellow ochre 54

Zebrawood 33
Zinc stearates 92

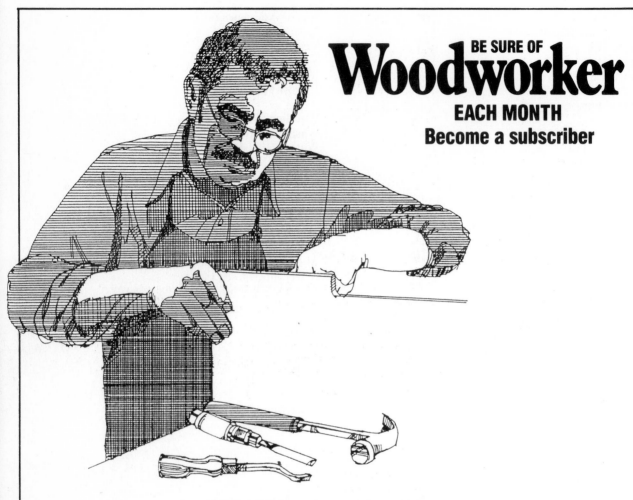